MEL BAY'S COMPLETE BANJO BOOK

By Neil Griffin

Contents

New Orleans Blues

(Tuning: GDGBD)

Key: a minor

Arr. by: Karl Kurth

Slow, with a beat

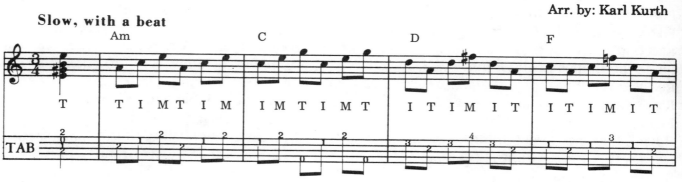

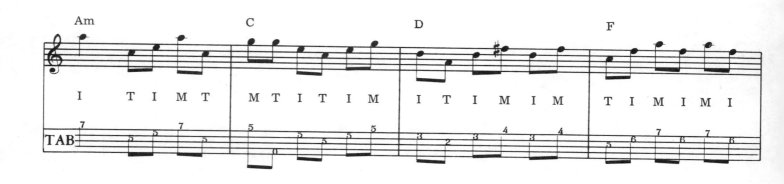

(Modulation)

5

Wildwood Flower

(Tuning: GDGBD)

Arr. by: Karl Kurth

Yankee Doodle

(Tuning: GDGBD)

Fairly Bright Tempo

Arr. by: Karl Kurth

✱ easier than using 2

Jesse James

(G Tuning)

Traditional Folk Song
Arr. by: Karl Kurth

8

Chorus

John Hardy

(G Tuning)

Arr. by: Karl Kurth

Snappy Tempo

Bile 'Dat Cabbage

(C Tuning — GCGBD)

Moderately

Arr. by: Karl Kurth

11

Old Joe Clark

(G Tuning)

Brightly
(Watch the thumb in R.H.)

Arr. by: Karl Kurth

Amazing Grace

(G Tuning)

Arr. by: Karl Kurth

Blow Ye Winds

(G Tuning)

Bright Tempo

Arr. by: Karl Kurth

Cindy

(C Tuning GCGBD)

Arr. by: Karl Kurth

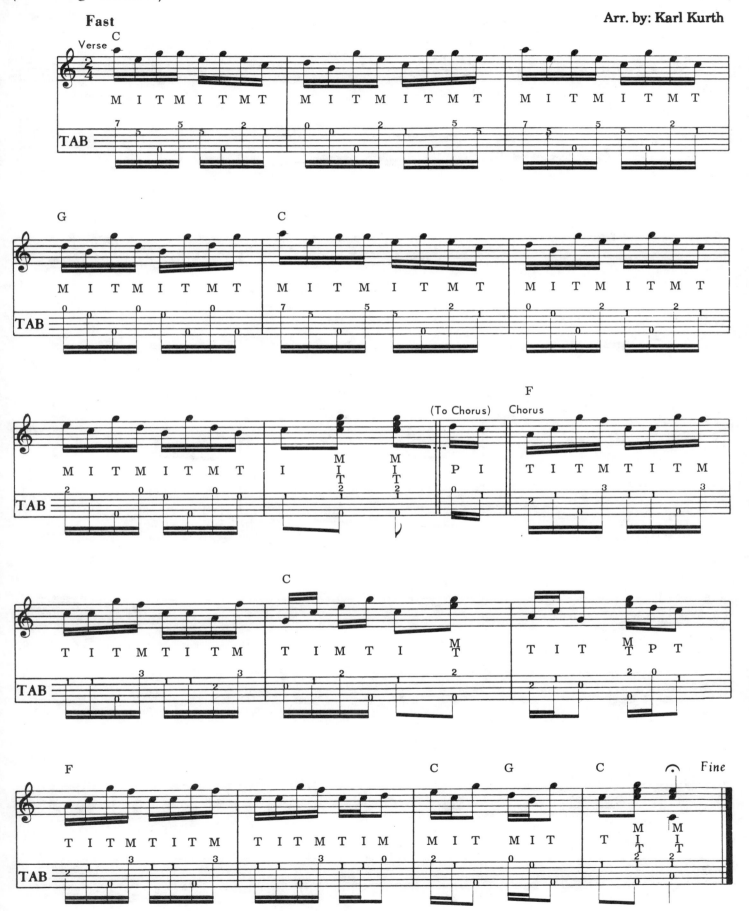

Lonesome Road

(D Tuning: ADF#AD)

Arr. by: Karl Kurth

16

Fire Water

by Karl Kurth

G Tuning

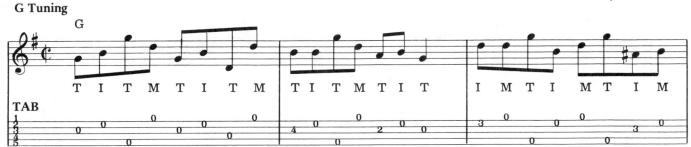

Worried Man Blues

(G Tuning)

Moderately Fast

Traditional
Arr. by: Karl Kurth

18

The Drunken Sailor

(GDGBD)

(a second position study)

Arr. by: Karl Kurth

This Train

(G Tuning)

Watch those hammers and pull offs.

Gentle Gospel Swing

Arr. by: Karl Kurth

Dixie

(G Tuning)

Arr. by: Karl Kurth

Spirited

* Barre using two fingers

Shady Grove / Lonesome Traveler Medley

(G minor Tuning: GDGB♭D)

Arr. by: Karl Kurth

Crawdad Song

Bright and Humorous (Folk Style)

Arr. by: Karl Kurth

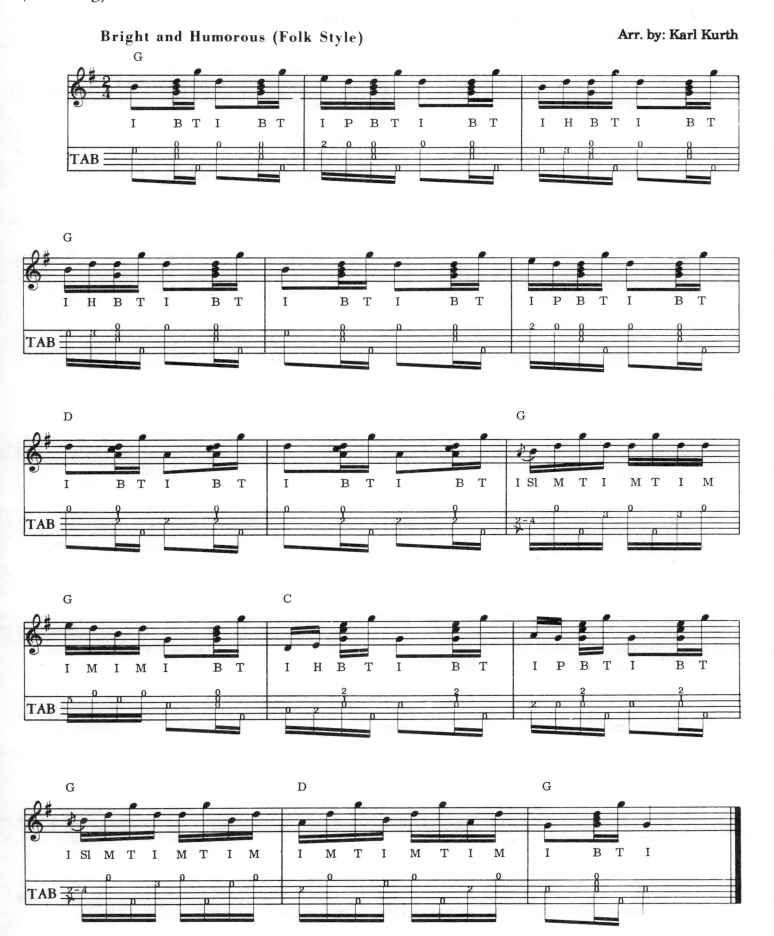

23

Skip to My Lou

(C Tuning: GCGBD)

Spirited Hoedown Tempo

Arr. by: Karl Kurth

Variation with double thumbing

Brady and Duncan

(G Tuning)

Arr. by: Karl Kurth

Brisk Tempo

Cory Cory

(G Tuning) **Bluegrass** Arr. by: Karl Kurth

John Henry

(G Tuning)

Arr. by: Karl Kurth

Sourwood Mountain

G,D,G,B,D

Arr. by: Neil Griffin

Poor Ellen Smith

G D G B D

Arr. by: Neil Griffin

Buffalo Gals

G D G B D

Arr. by: Neil Griffin

Camptown Races

Arr. by: Neil Griffin

Sail Away Ladies

Arr. by: Neil Griffin

Greensleeves

Arr. by: Neil Griffin

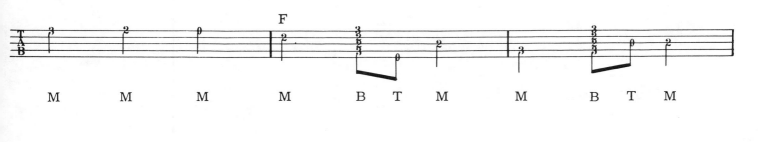

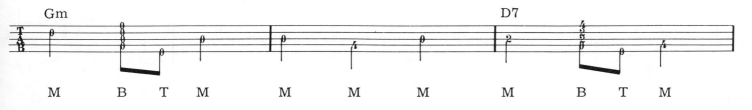

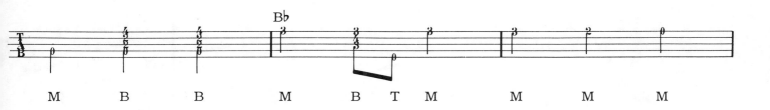

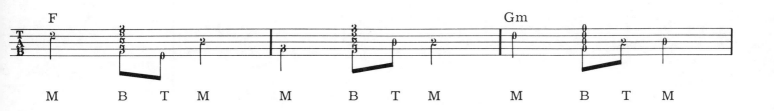

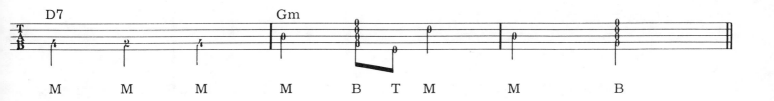

Judgment Day

G D G Bb D

By: Neil Griffin

Jamestown

G D G B♭ D

Arr. by: Neil Griffin

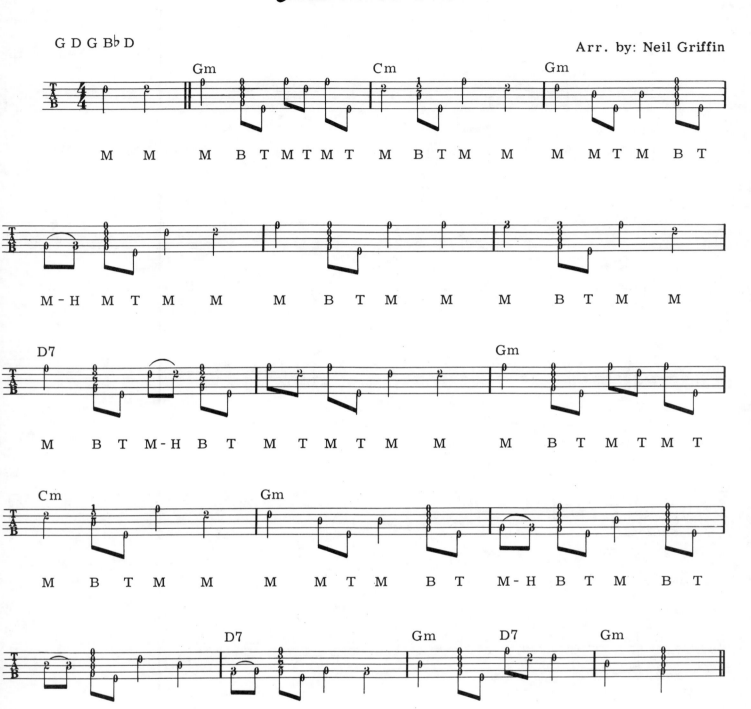

Oh Susanna

Arr. by: Neil Griffin

Sally Goodin'

G D G B D

Arr. by: Neil Griffin

37

Cumberland Gap

Arr. by: Neil Griffin

Where Shall I Be?

G C G C E

Arr. by: Neil Griffin

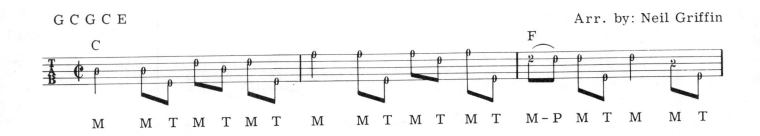

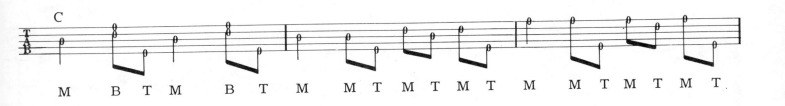

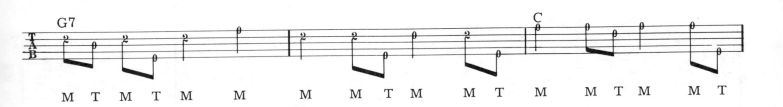

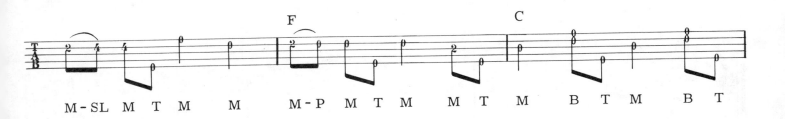

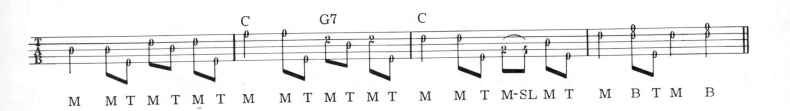

Black-Eyed Susie

Arr. by: Neil Griffin

Shortnin' Bread

Arr. by: Neil Griffin

41

Chicken Reel

Johnny Booker

G D G B D

Arr. by: Neil Griffin

NOTE: The first half of this solo is played in the "2- finger style, the second half uses roll number 7.

Omie Wise

GDGBD

Arr. by: Neil Griffin

44

East Virginia

Arr. by: Neil Griffin

G D G B D

Little Birdie

G D G B D

Arr. by: Neil Griffin

Julida Polka

Arr. by: Neil Griffin

Aura Lee

G D G B D

Arr. by: Neil Griffin

Little Maggie

GDGBD

Arr. by: Neil Griffin

Lonesome Valley

G D G B D

Arr. by: Neil Griffin

Jubalo

A D G B D

Arr. by: Neil Griffin

Mississippi Sawyer

Arr. by: Neil Griffin

The White Cockade

G D G B D

Arr. by: Neil Griffin

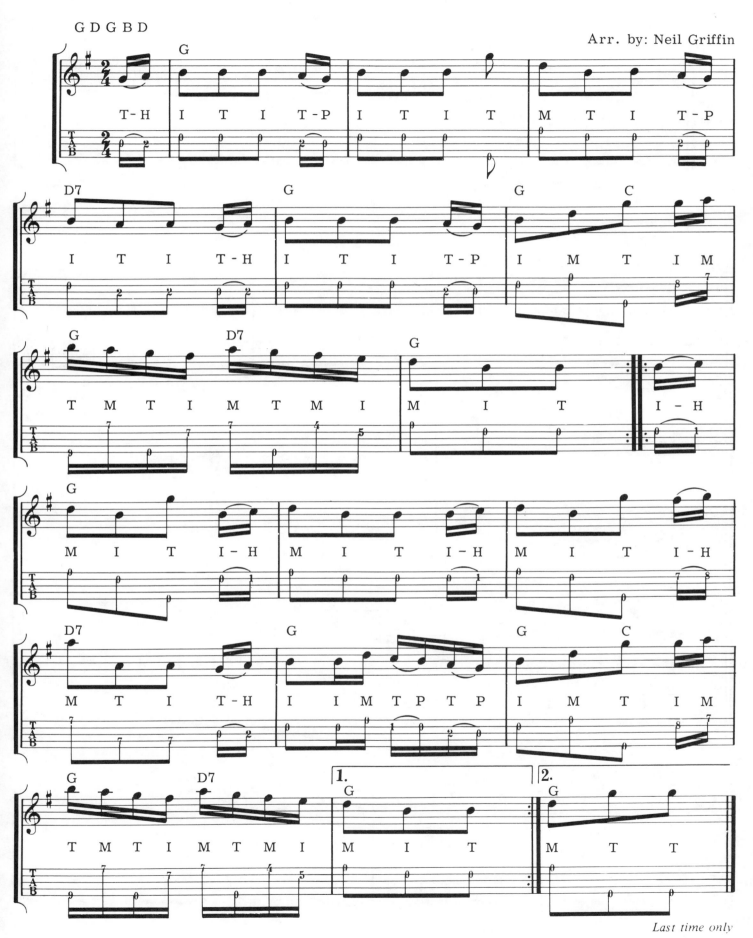

Last time only

Buckwheat Batter

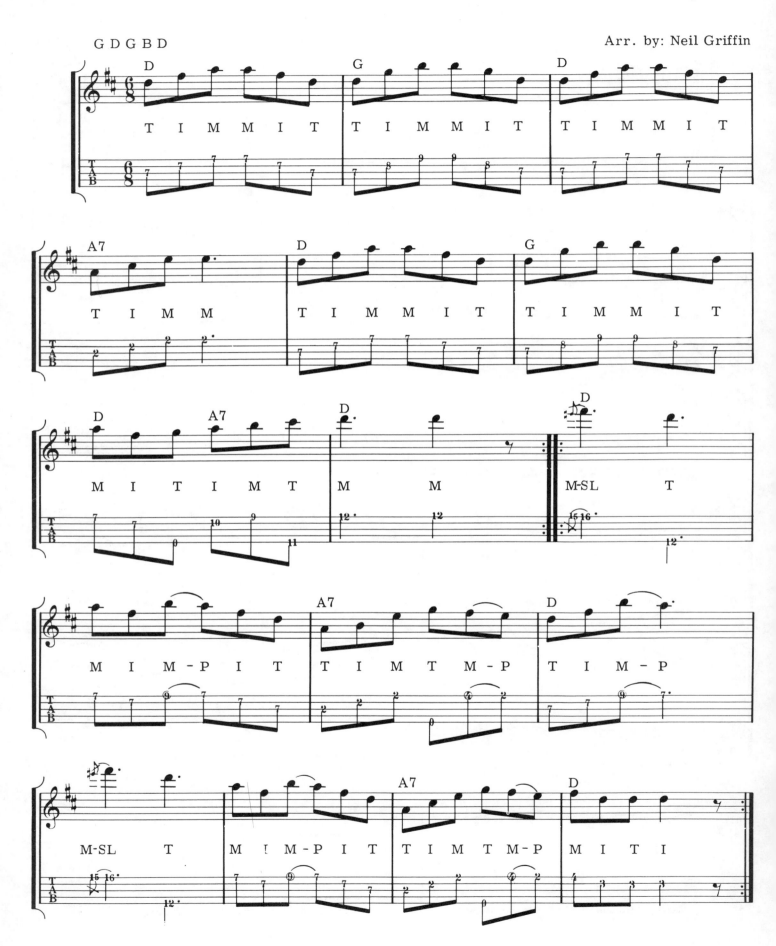

Money Musk

A D G B D

Arr. by: Neil Griffin

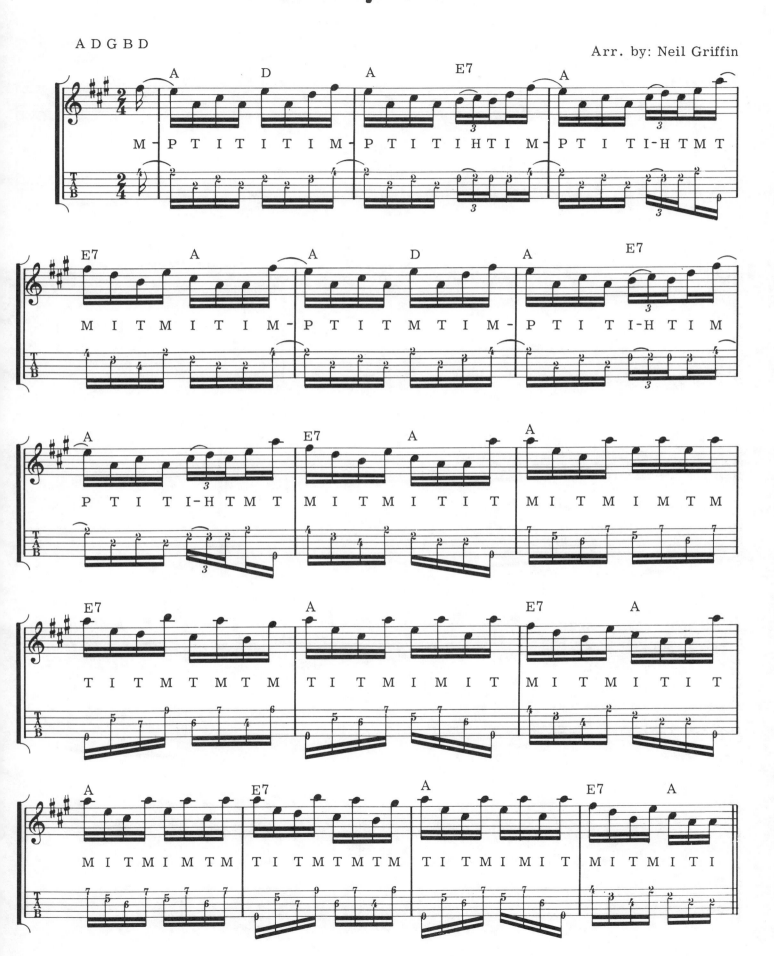

Ocean Waves

Arr. by: Neil Griffin

Happy Jack

Yonder She Goes

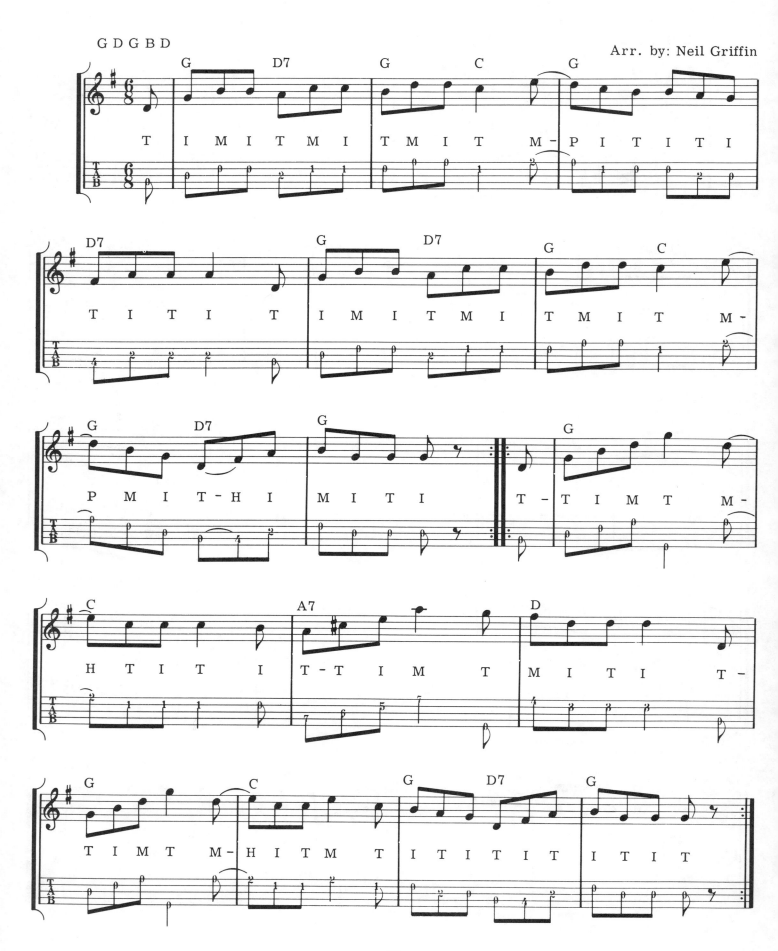

Murphy's Bird

Chicken Stampede

Arr. by: Neil Griffin

G D G B D

Raccoon's Tail

G D G B D

Arr. by: Neil Griffin

61

Uncle Joe

Arr. by: Neil Griffin

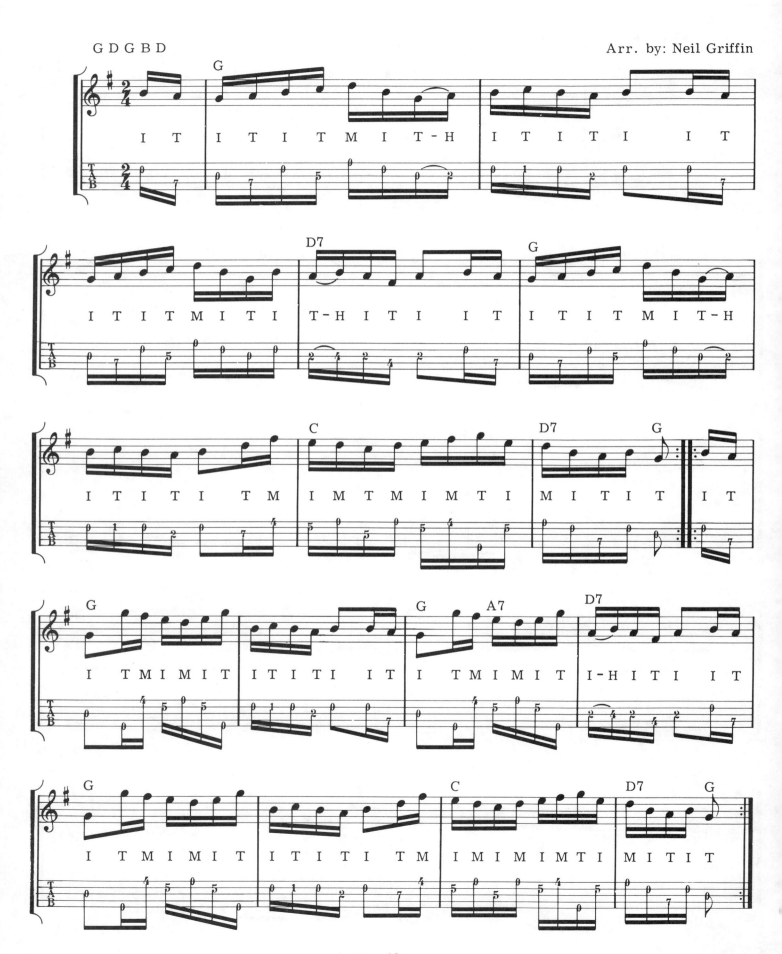

Arkansas Traveler

Traditional
Arranged by Carl Jackson

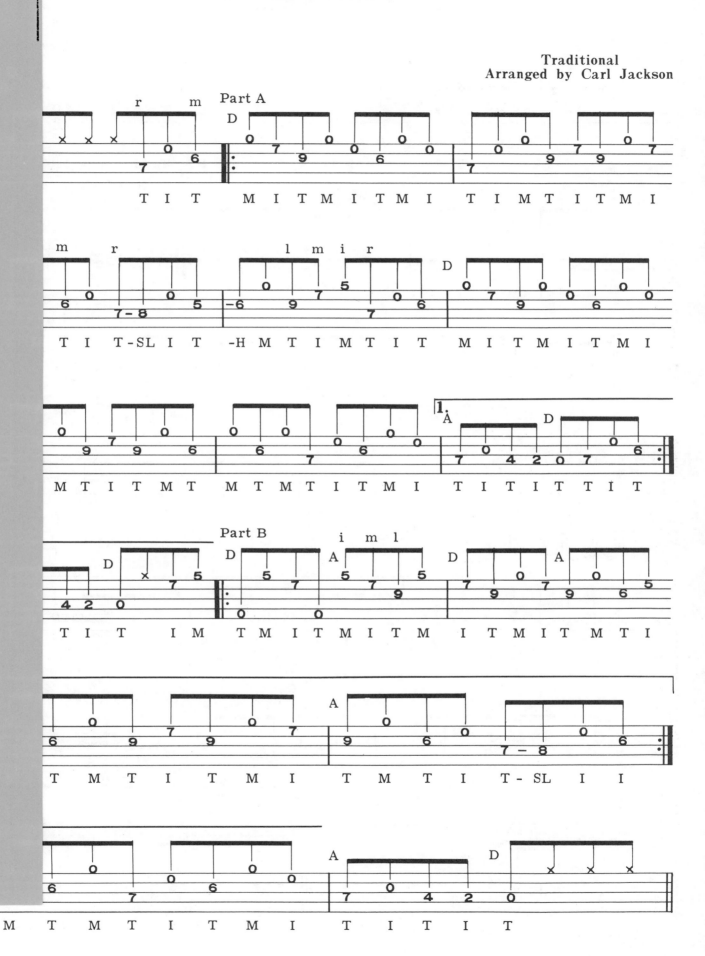

Cripple Creek

Traditional
Arranged by Carl Jackson

Key of G
Open G tuning

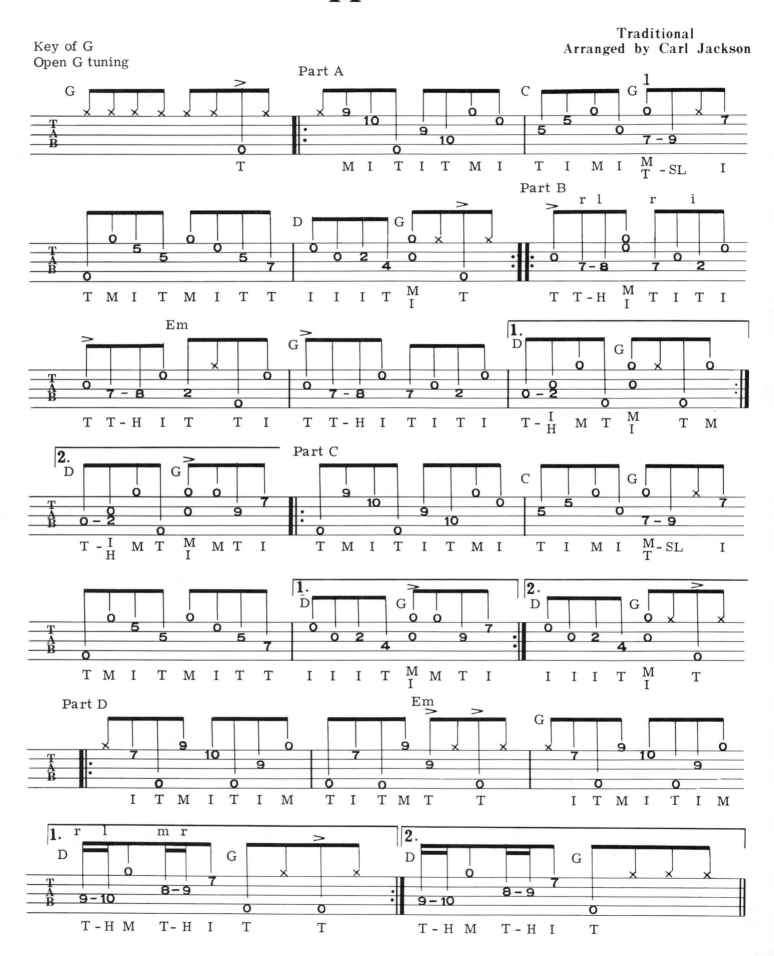

Flop-Eared Mule

Traditional
Arranged by Carl Jackson

Key of G
Open G tuning

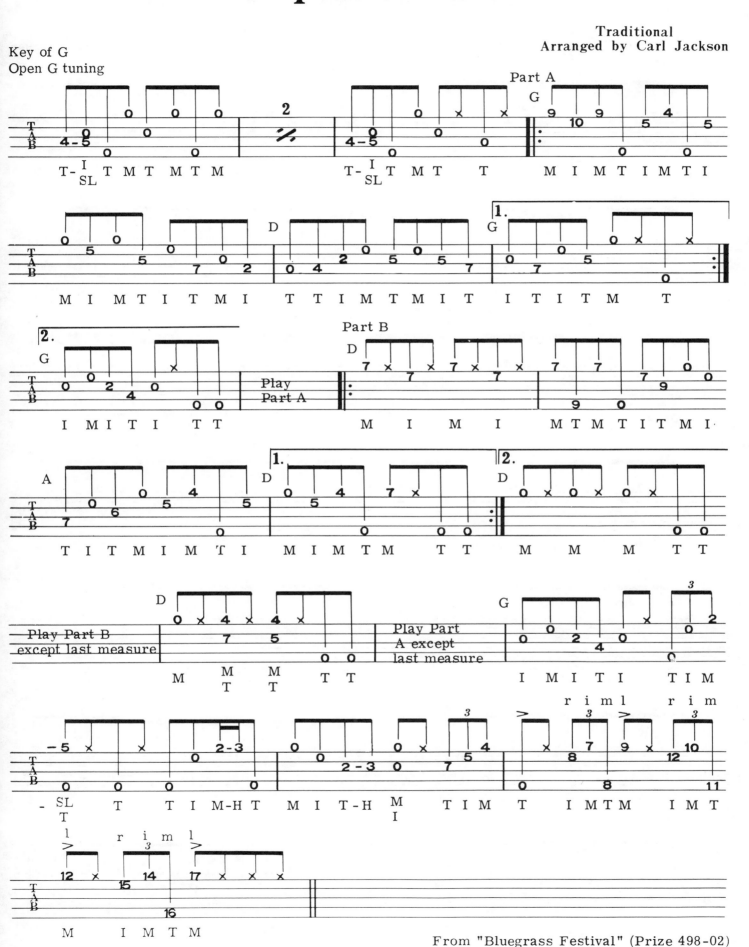

From "Bluegrass Festival" (Prize 498-02)

Done Gone

Key of G minor
Gm tuning, 5th string raised (see notes)

Traditional
Arranged by Carl Jackson

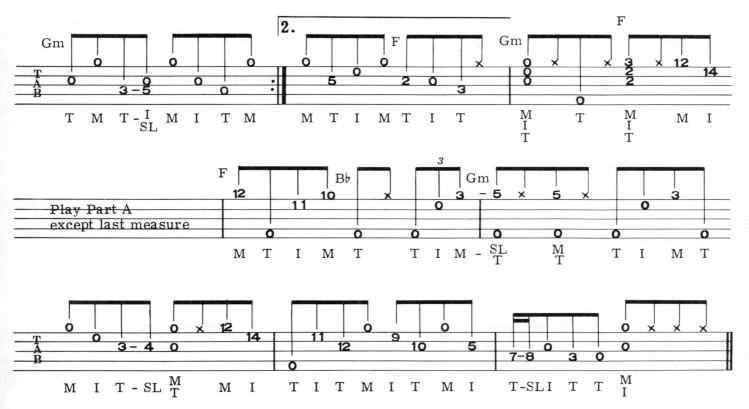

From "Bluegrass Festival" (Prize 498-02)

The tuning for "Done Gone" is a modified G minor, in which you start with regular G tuning and then lower the second string ½ tone to B flat; and then you raise the fifth string 3½ tones to a high B flat. But different banjos use different fifth-string capos; some have a sliding capo, some have H.O. railroad spikes, and some don't have any capo. The tablature is written for banjos having a spike in the neck at the 7th fret, so that to tune it for "Done Gone" you put the string under the spike and turn it up ½ tone.

If your banjo has a sliding capo, you wouldn't turn up the string, so you need to make a small change right on the page: On the fifth-string line, cross out "14" and write "15," and cross out "16" and write in "17." If your banjo has no fifth-string capo, you'd likely break the string turning it up all the way to B flat; but, if you want to try, then on the page cross out "14" on the fifth-string line and write in "12," and cross out "16" and write in "14."

67

Goodbye Liza Jane

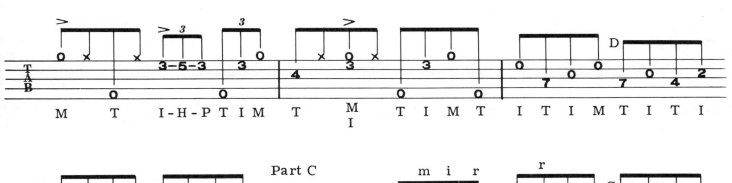

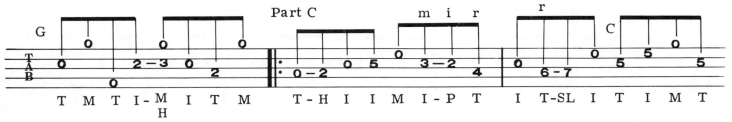

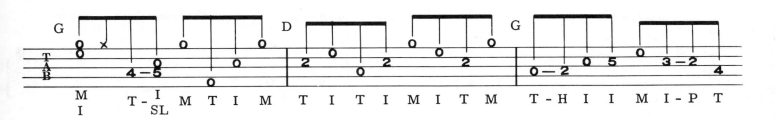

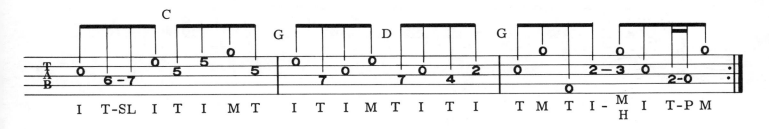

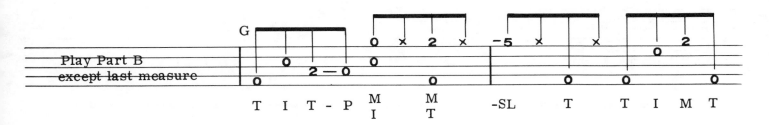

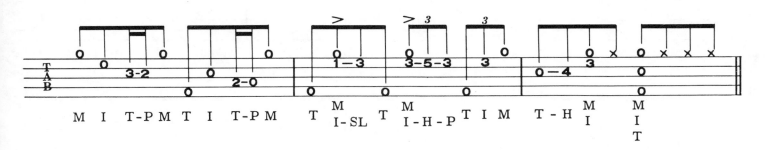

Say Old Man

Key of Em
G tuning, capo 2

Traditional
Arranged by Carl Jackson

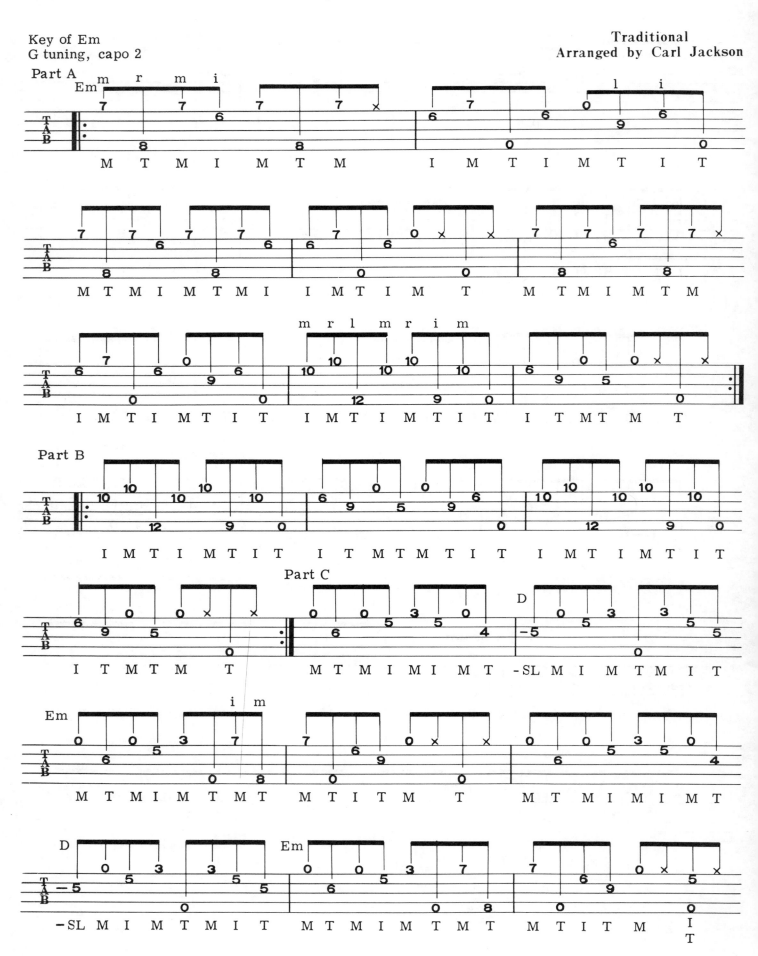

70

Part D

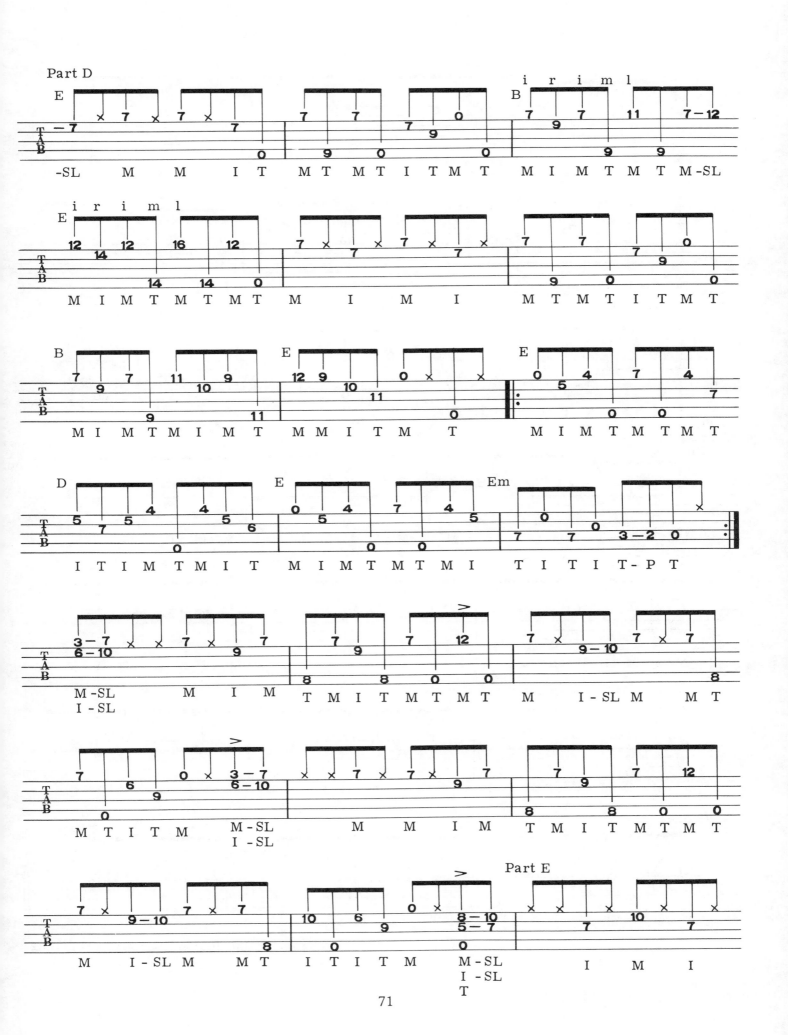

71

From "Banjo Player" (Capitol ST-11166)

The Girl I Left Behind Me

Arr by: Neil Griffin

Sailor's Hornpipe

Arr by: Neil Griffin

Devil's Dream

Arr by: Neil Griffin

Irish Washerwoman

Arr by: Neil Griffin

Garry Owen Jig

Arr by: Neil Griffin

Eighth of January

Arr by: Neil Griffin

Rick's Reel

By: Neil Griffin

Cock and Hen

Arr. by: Neil Griffin

The Keepsake

Arr. by: Neil Griffin

Blue-Eyed Maid

Arr. by: Neil Griffin

Red Fox

Arr. by: Neil Griffin

Wearing of the Green

Arr. by: Neil Griffin

84

Planxty George Brabazon

Arr. by: Neil Griffin

Pretty Fair Maid Jig

Arr. by: Neil Griffin

Rattle the Bottles Reel

Arr. by: Neil Griffin

Muldoon's Reel

Arr. by: Neil Griffin

88

Yellow-Hair'd Laddie Reel

Arr. by: Neil Griffin

89

Kilkenny Girl

Arr. by: Neil Griffin

The Bridal Jig

Arr. by: Neil Griffin

Keel Row Reel

Arr. by: Neil Griffin

Seven-Up Reel

Arr. by: Neil Griffin

Honeymoon Reel

Arr. by: Neil Griffin

Fill Up the Bowl Reel

Arr. by: Neil Griffin

Roving Bachelor Reel

Arr. by: Neil Griffin

Boys of Bockhill Jig

Arr. by: Neil Griffin

Joys of Wedlock Jig

Arr. by: Neil Griffin

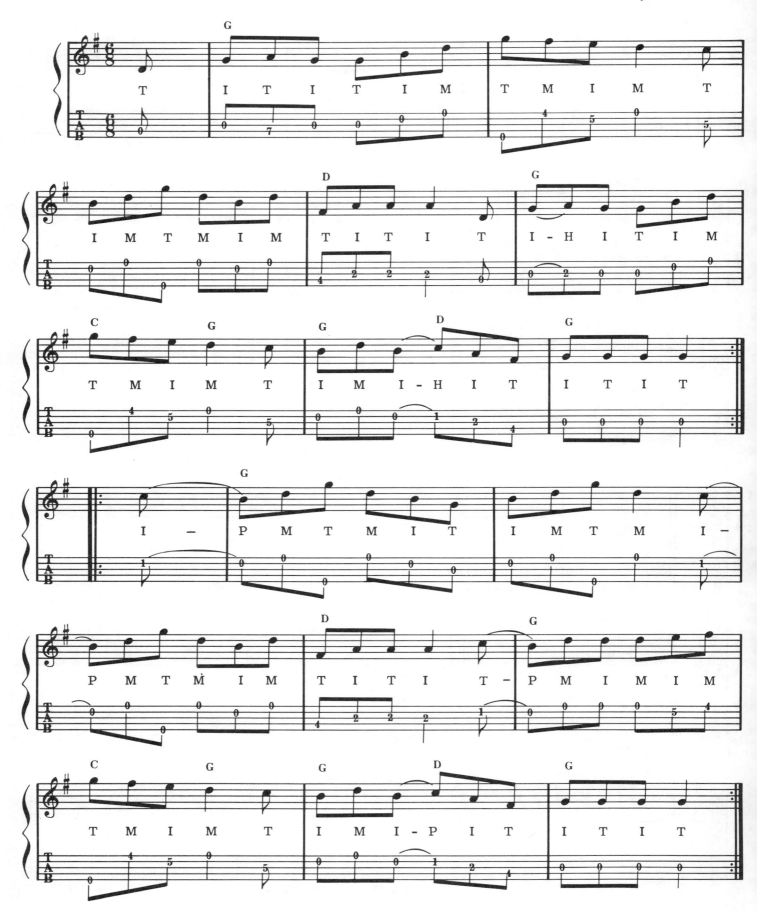

A Visit to Ireland

Arr. by: Neil Griffin

St. Patrick's Day Jig

Arr. by: Neil Griffin

Dusty Bob's Jig

Arr. by: Neil Griffin

Irish-American Jig

Arr. by: Neil Griffin

Whiskey Before Breakfast

Arr. by: Neil Griffin

One-Legged Man

Arr. by: Neil Griffin

Fine

D.C. al Fine

Soldier's Joy

Arr by: Neil Griffin

Rickett's Hornpipe

Arr by: Neil Griffin

Witch of the Wave Reel

Arr by: Neil Griffin

Neil's Reel

Arr by: NEIL GRIFFI

108

Smoky House

Arr. by: Neil Griffin

Nora O'Neill

Arr. by: Neil Griffin

Liberty

Arr by: Neil Griffin

Turkey in the Straw

Arr by: Neil Griffin

112

Golden Slippers

Arr by: Neil Griffin

113

Paddy Whack Jig

Arr by: Neil Griffin

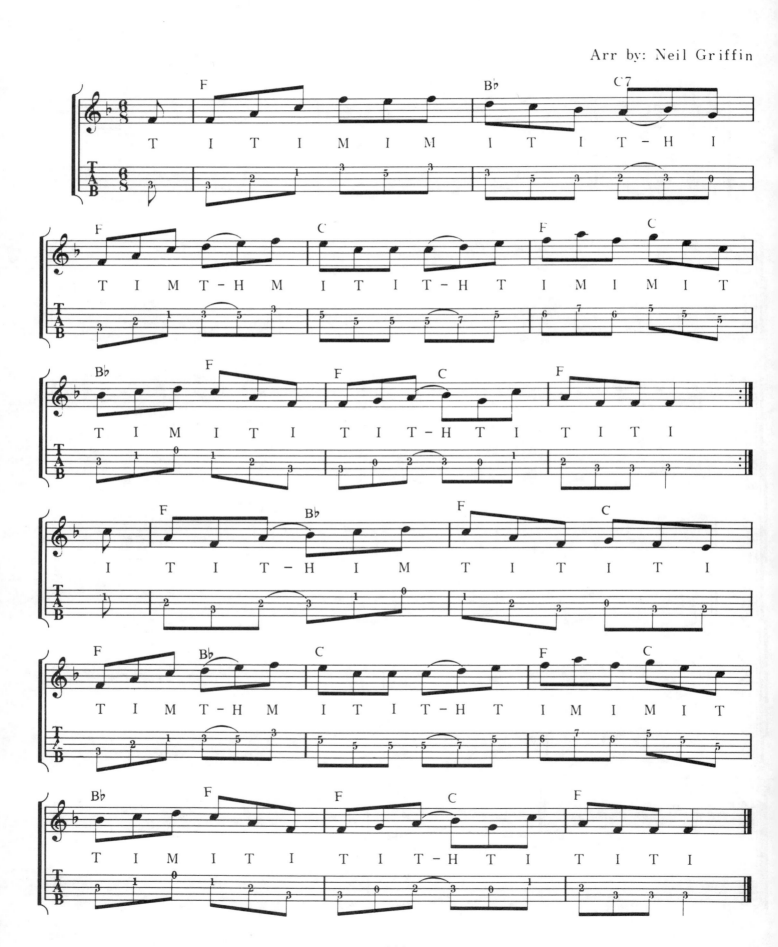

Miss McCleod's Reel

Arr by: Neil Griffin

Blue Mountain Train

Arr.by:Neil Griffin

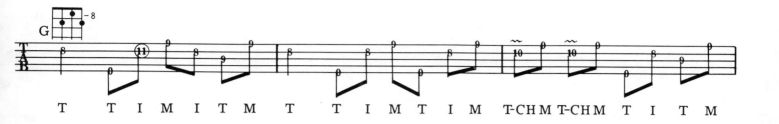
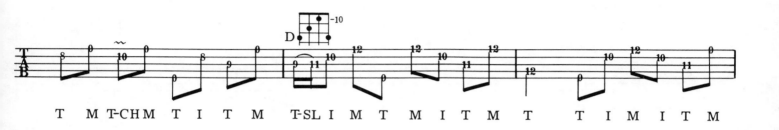
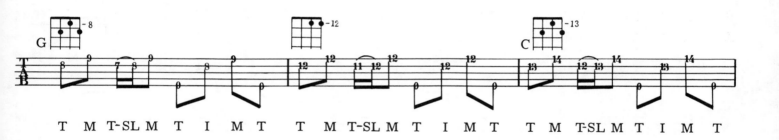
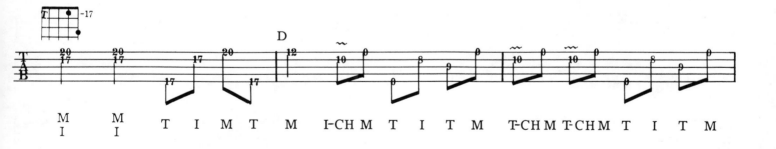

Chime Time

By: Neil Griffin

Georgia Gallop

by: Neil Griffin

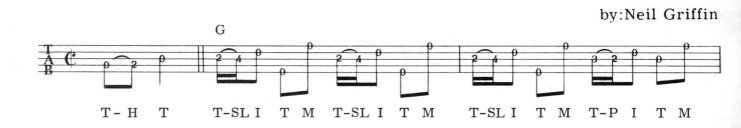

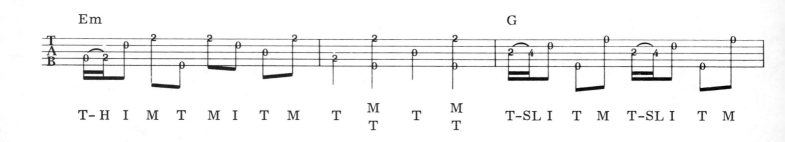

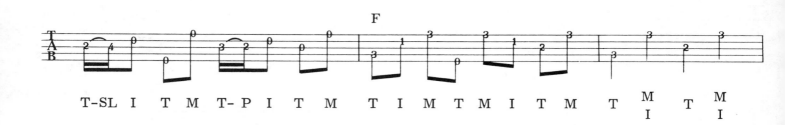

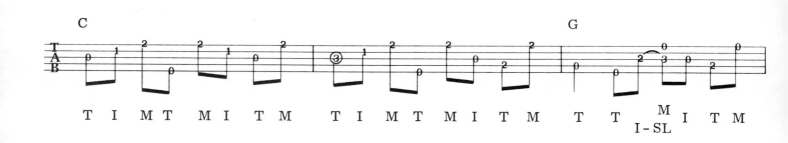

Fire on the Mountain

Arr by: Neil Griffin

Pickin' Around

By: Neil Griffin

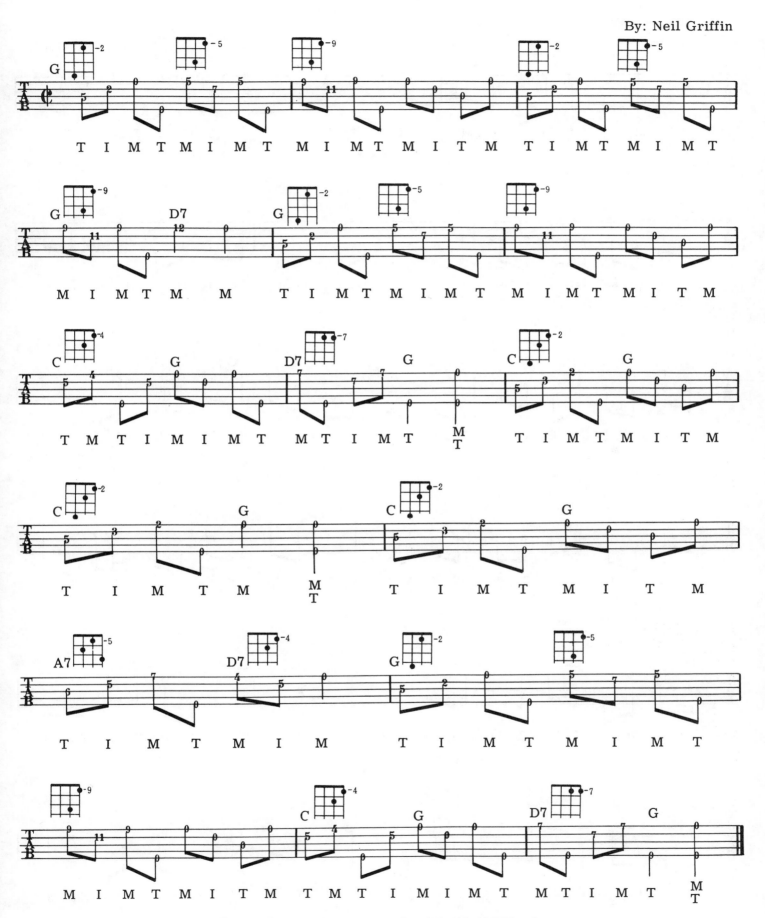

Bury Me Beneath the Willow

Arr.by: Neil Griffin

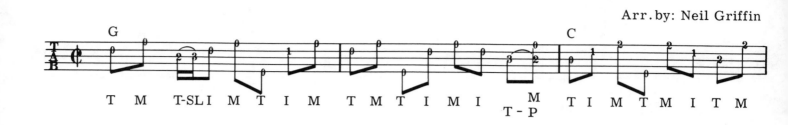

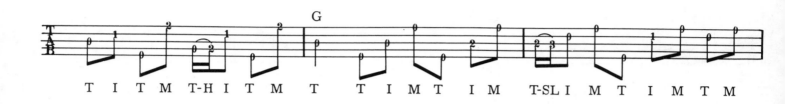

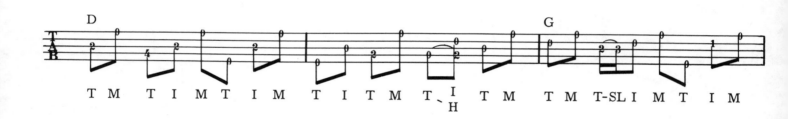

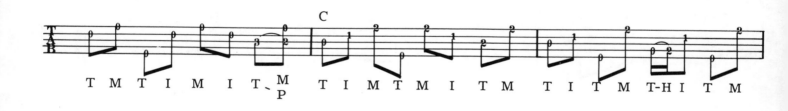

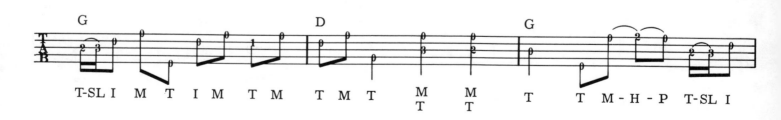

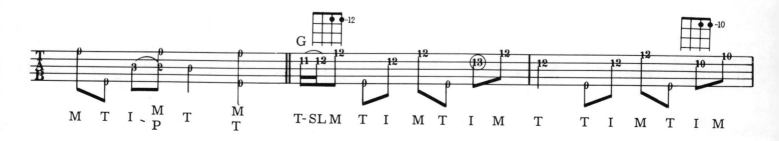

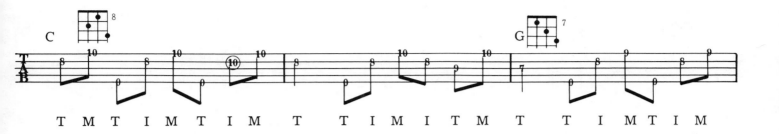
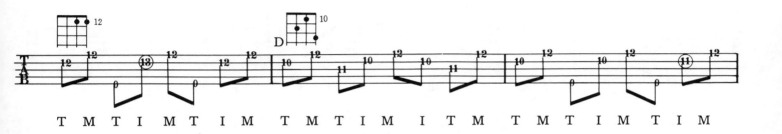
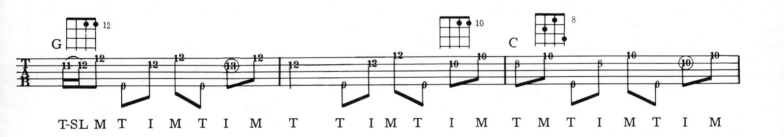
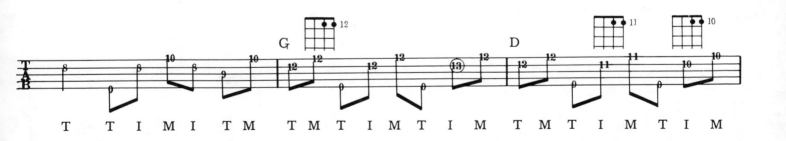
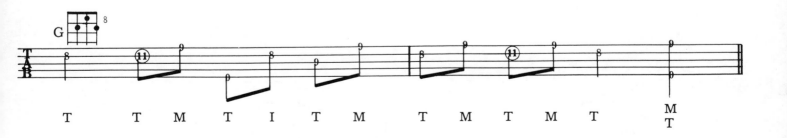

Will the Circle Be Unbroken

Arr. by: Neil Griffin

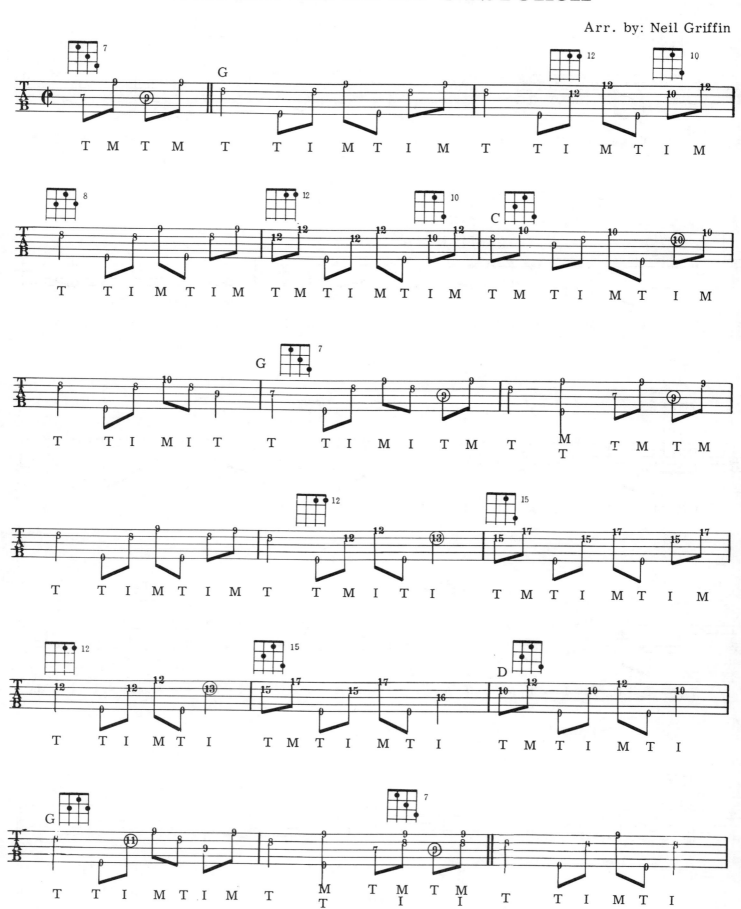

126

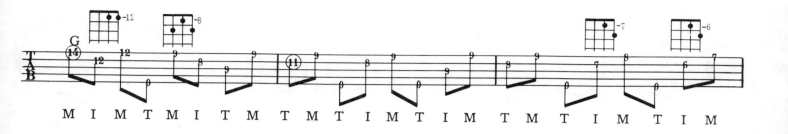

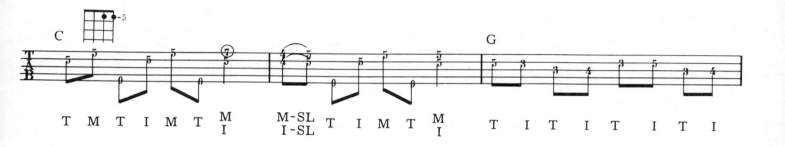

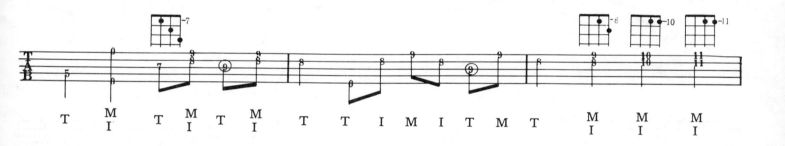

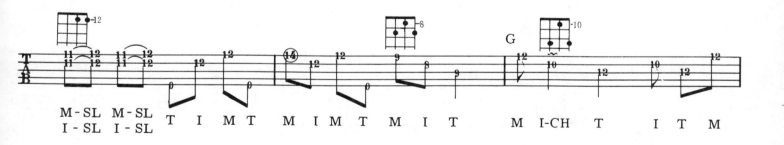

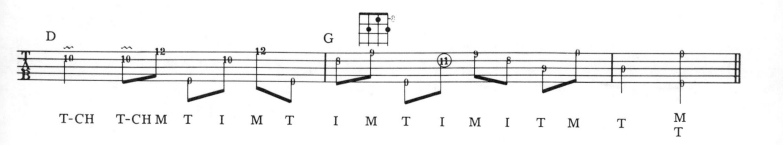

127

Wabash Cannonball

Arr. by: Neil Griffin

Wreck of the Old 97

Arr. by: Neil Griffin

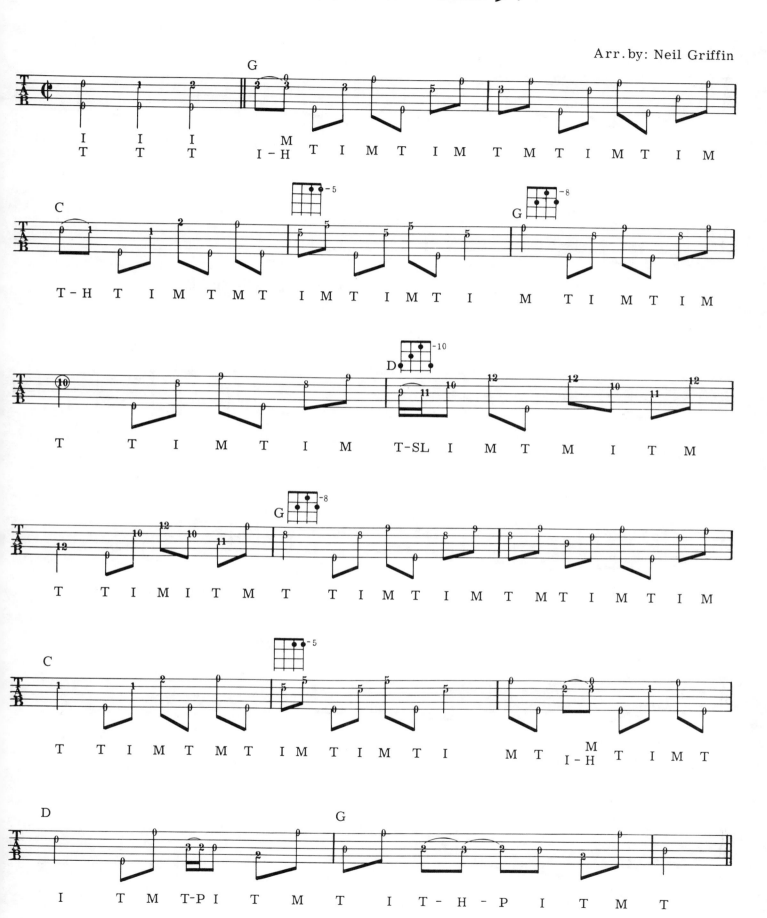

Nine-Pound Hammer

Arr. by: Neil Griffin

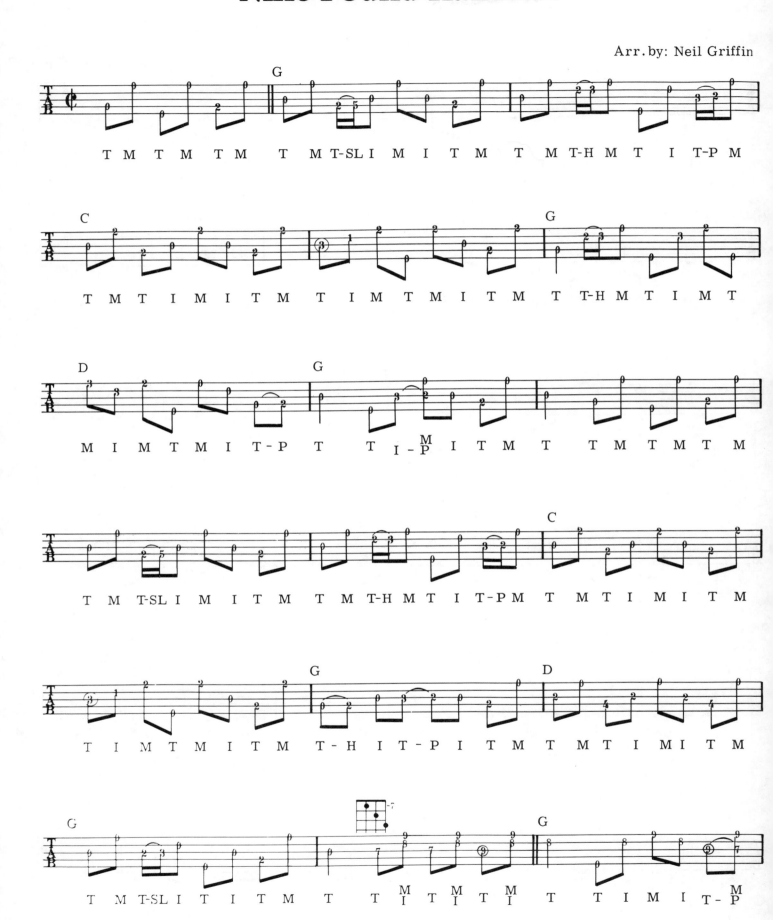

130

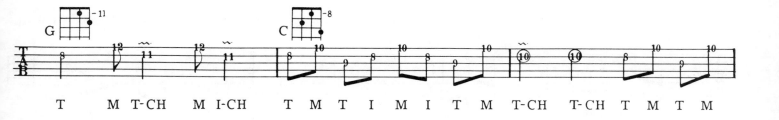

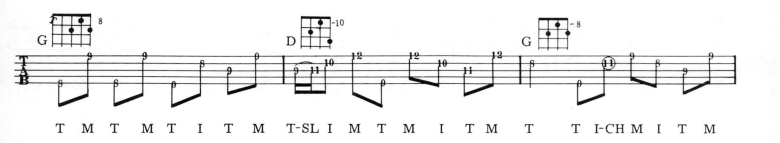

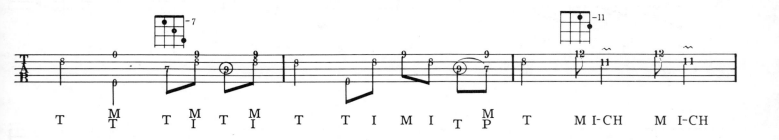

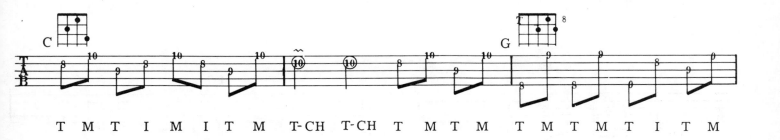

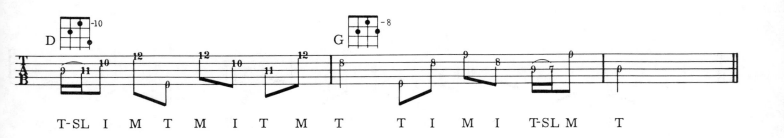

Carry Me Back to Old Virginia

Arr. by: Neil Griffin

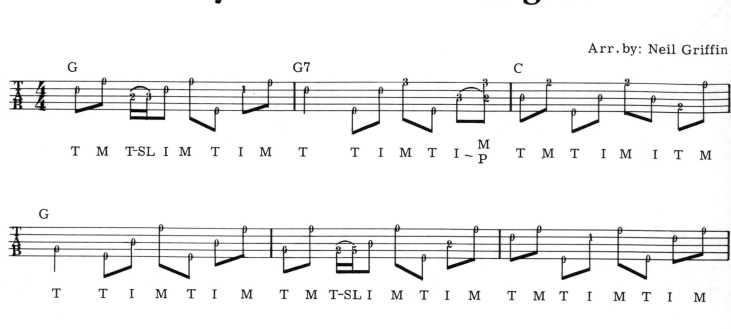

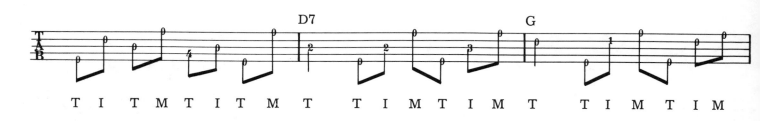

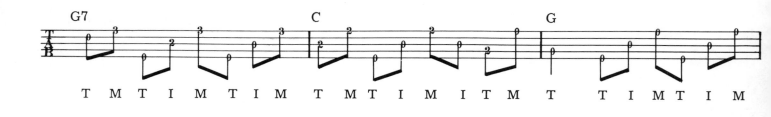

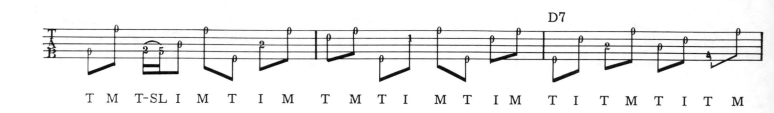

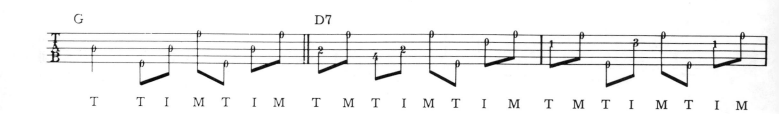

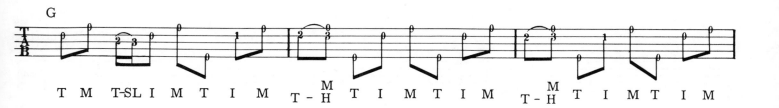

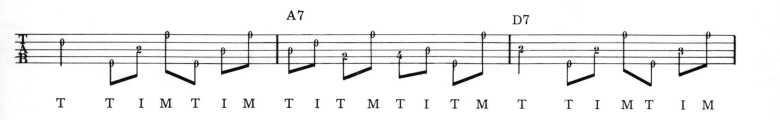

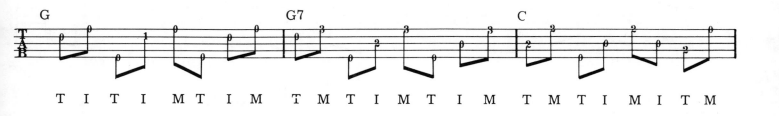

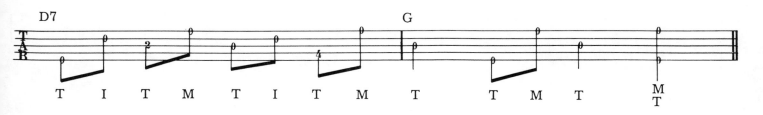

Banjo Blues

By: Neil Griffin

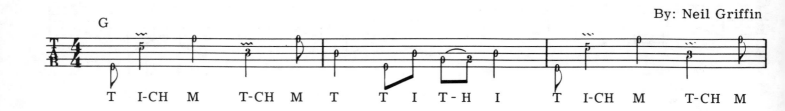

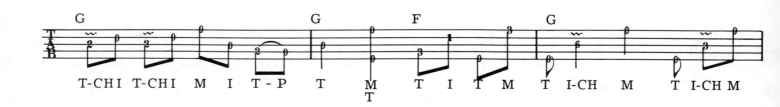

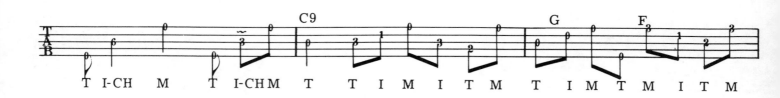

134

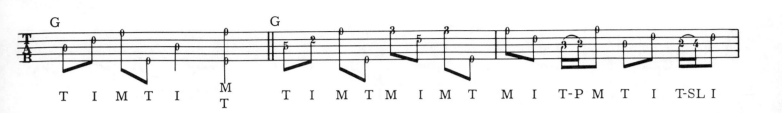

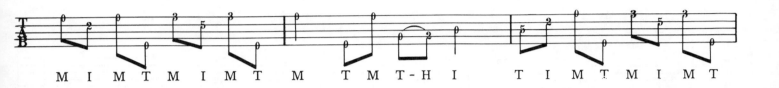

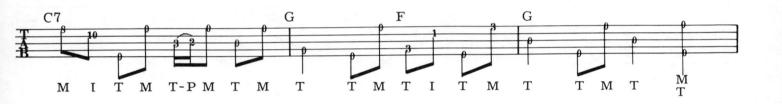

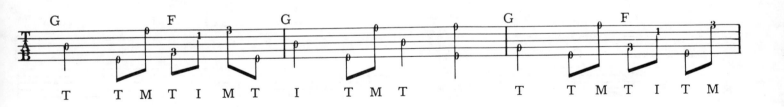

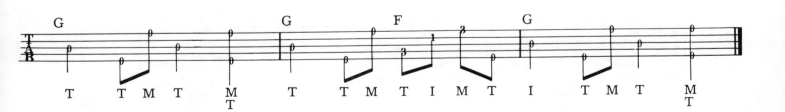

Bluegrass Joe

Arr. by: Neil Griffin

Mama Don't 'Low

Arr. by: Neil Griffin

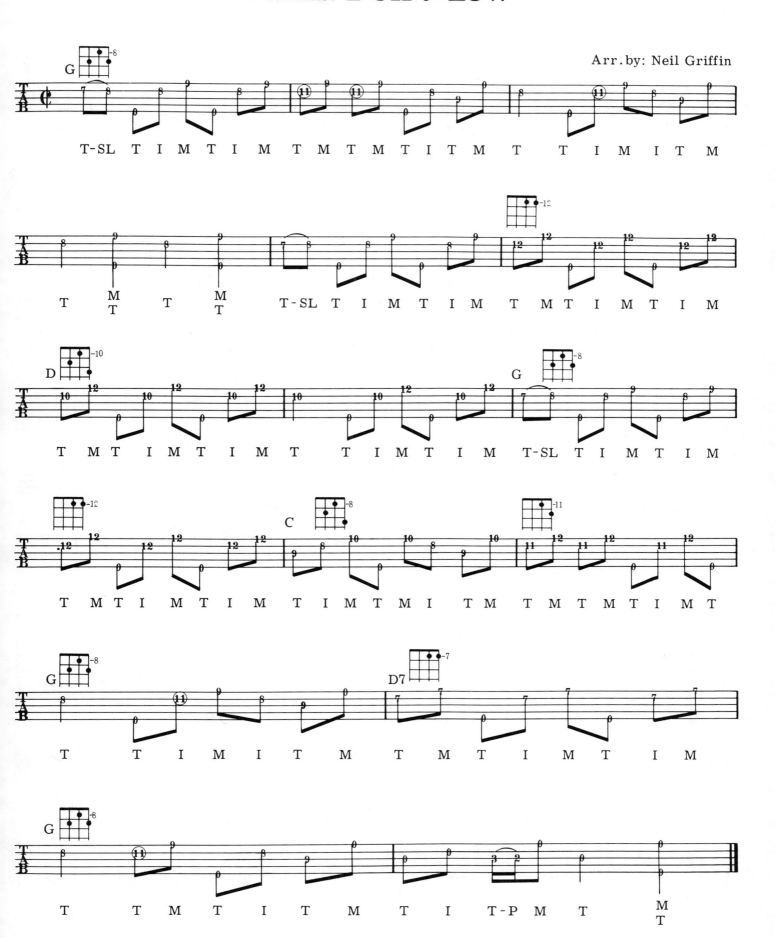

Stockade Blues

Arr.by: Neil Griffin

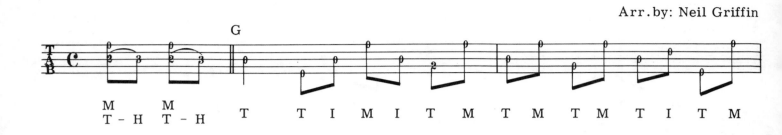

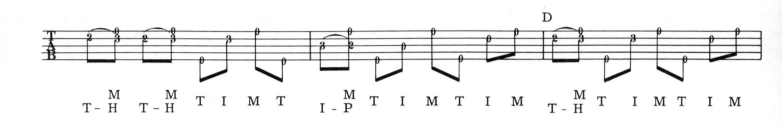

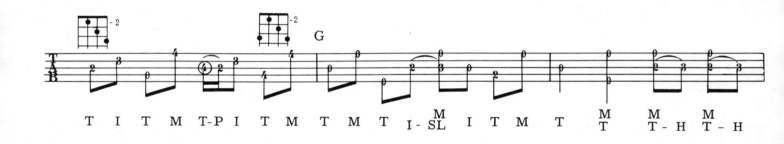

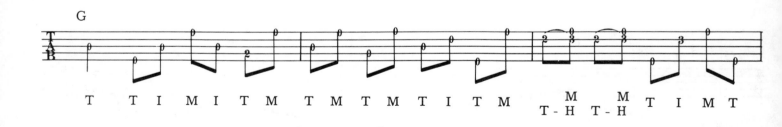

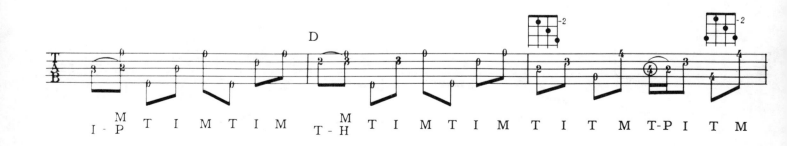

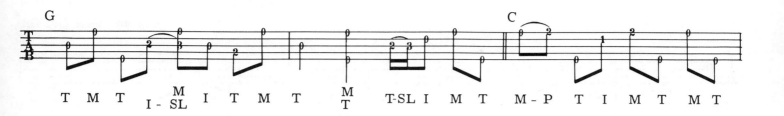

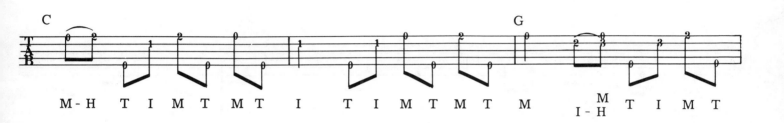

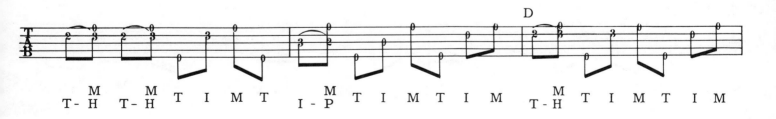

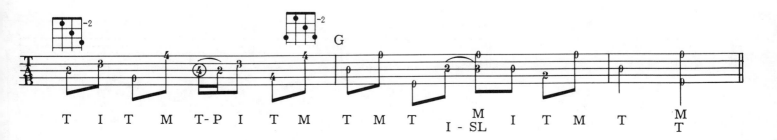

Salty Dog

Arr.by: Neil Griffin

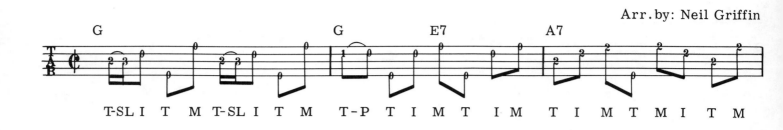

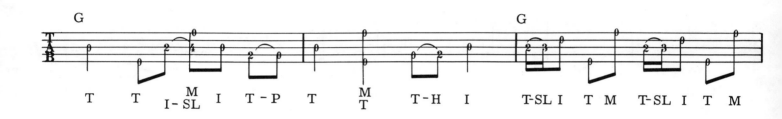

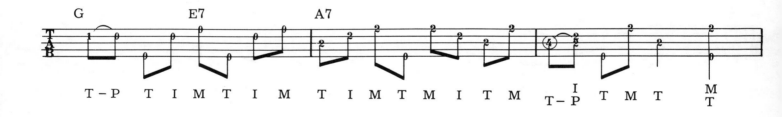

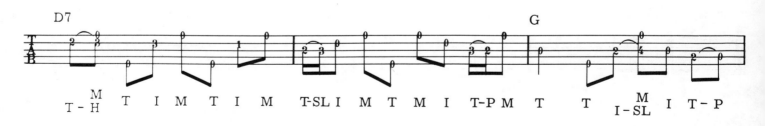

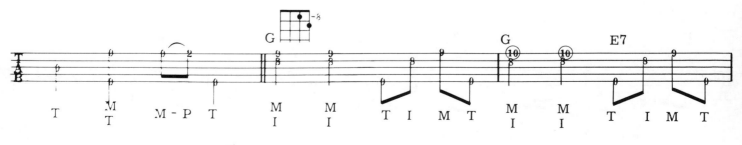

Fine

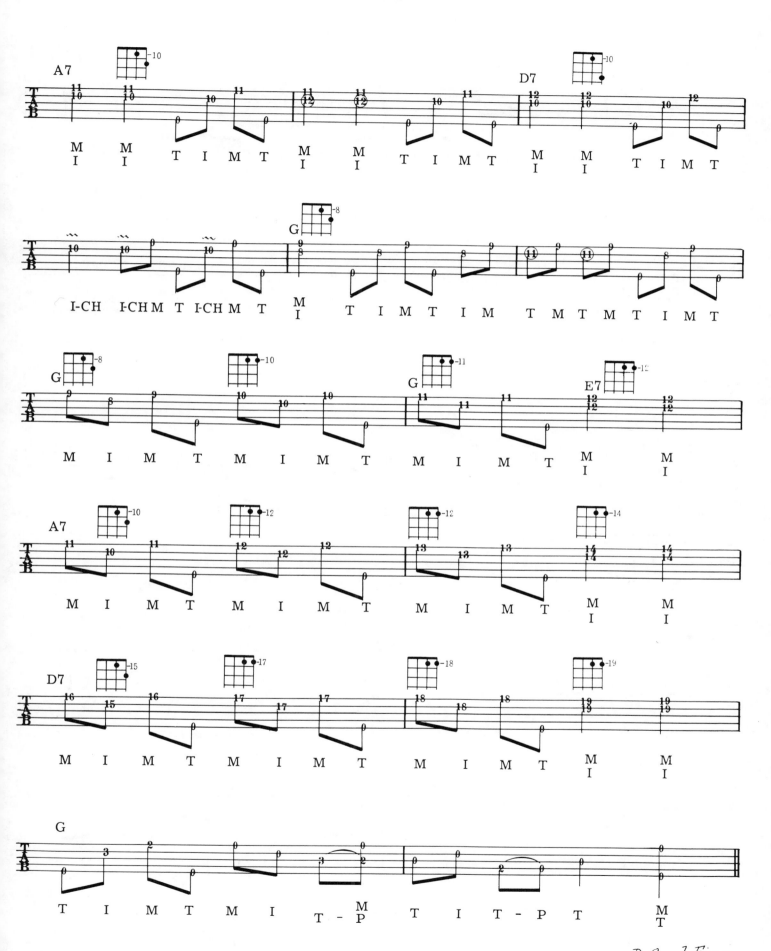

D.C. al Fine

Catfish Creek

Arr. by: Neil Griffin

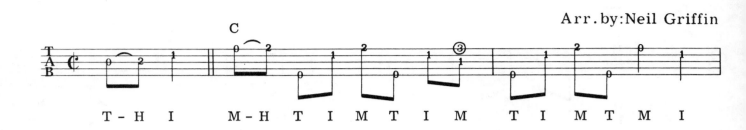

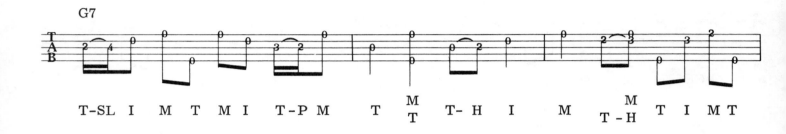

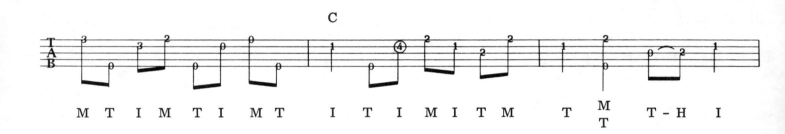

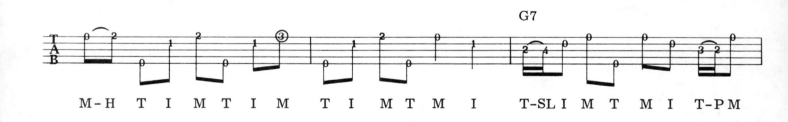

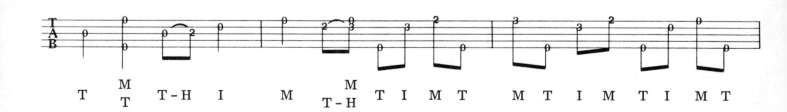

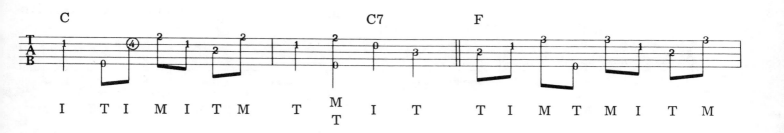

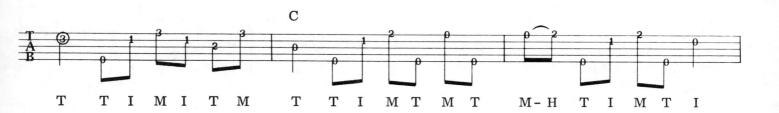

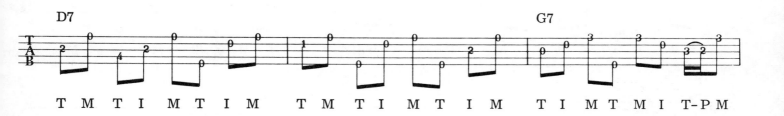

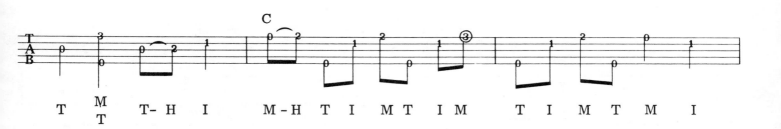

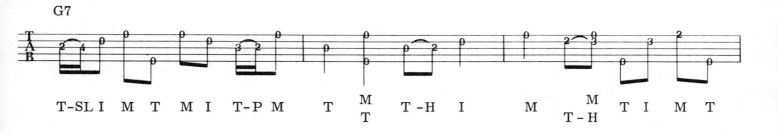

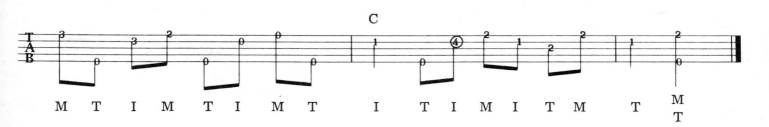

Grandfather's Clock

Arr. by: Neil Griffin

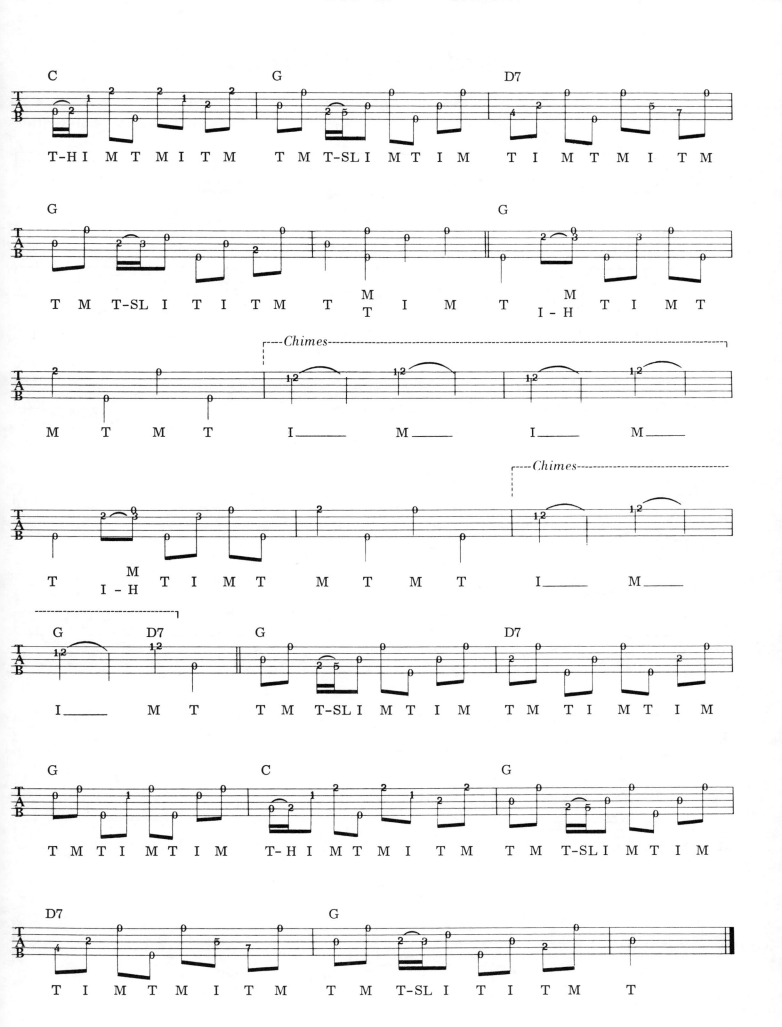

Frankie and Johnny

Arr. by: Neil Griffin

Careless Love

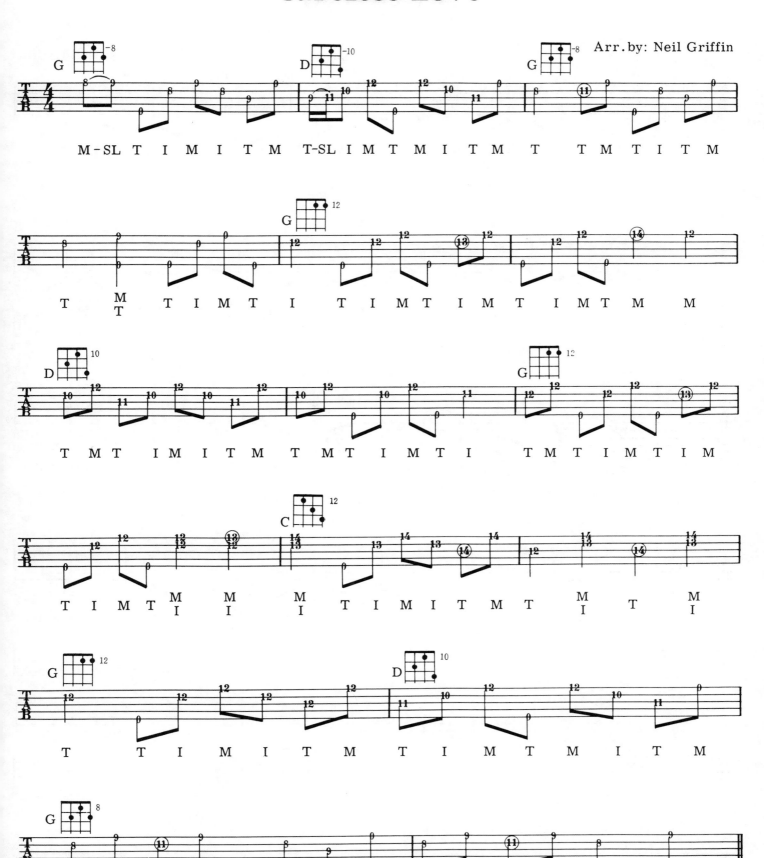

Bill Bailey

Arr. by: Neil Griffin

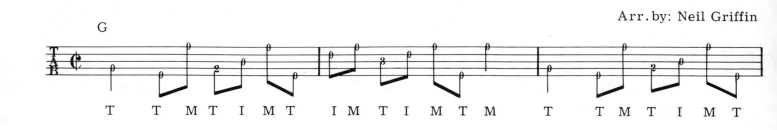

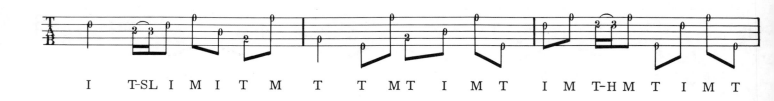

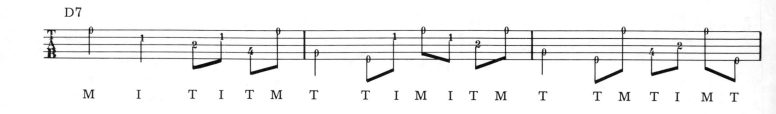

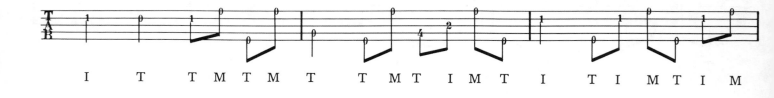

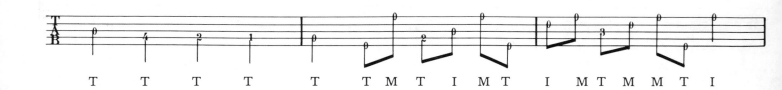

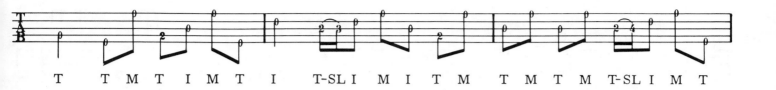

T   T M T I M T I   T-SL I M I T M   T M T M T-SL I M T

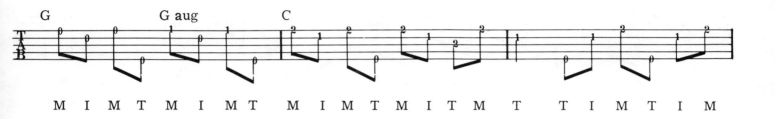

M I M T M I M T   M I M T M I T M   T   T I M T I M

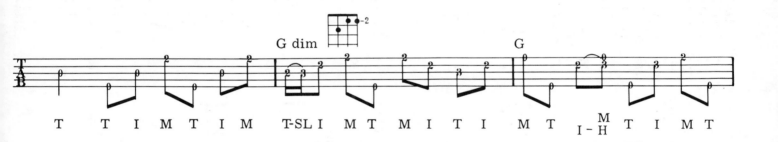

T   T I M T I M   T-SL I M T M I T I   M T I - M T I M T
                                                                  H

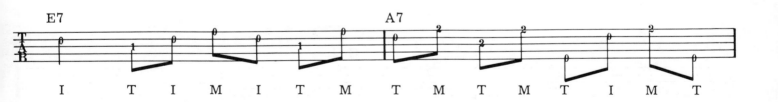

I   T I M I T M T M T M T I M T

I - M T I M I T - M T M T-SL I M T I M T I M I T M
H   P   T

Hard and It's Hard

Arr.by: Neil Griffin

Old Time Religion

Arr. by: Neil Griffin

Bully of the Town

Arr.by: Neil Griffin

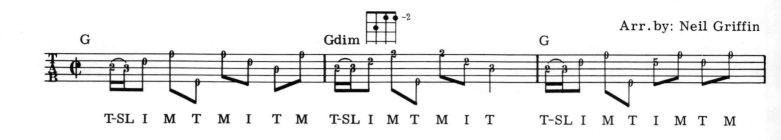

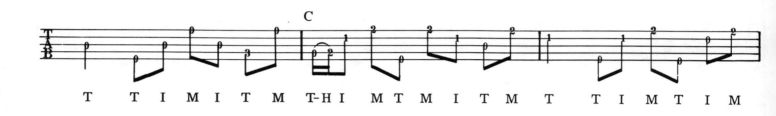

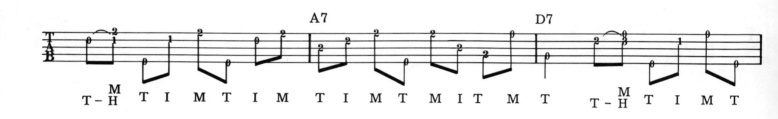

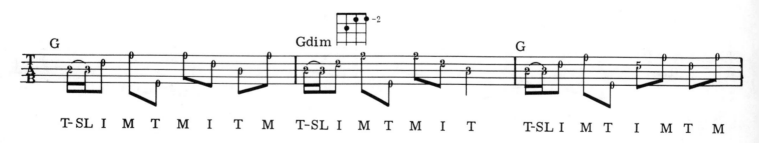

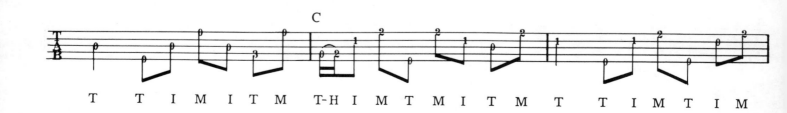

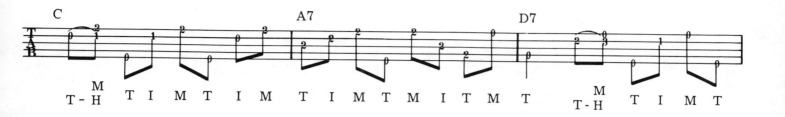

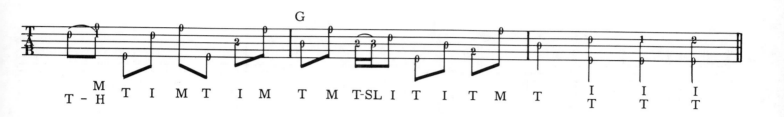

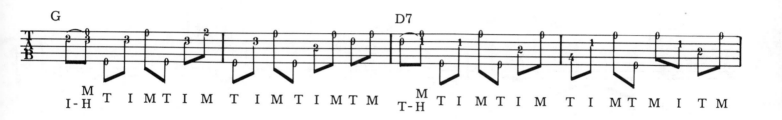

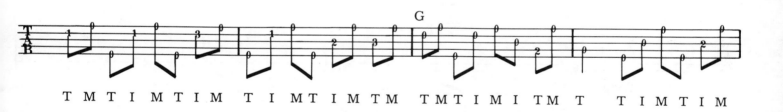

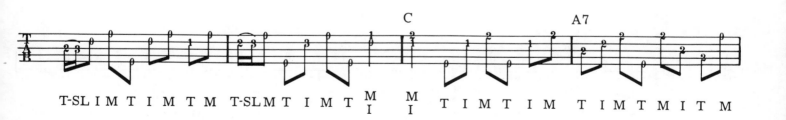

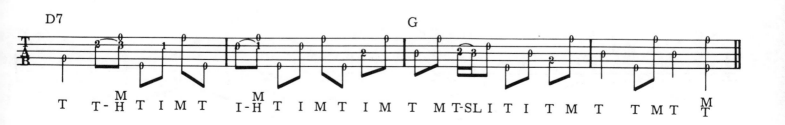

Bicentennial Breakdown

by: Neil Griffin

Intro - Slow and Stately

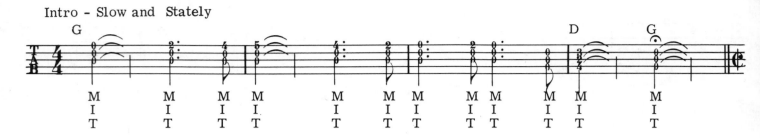

Fast

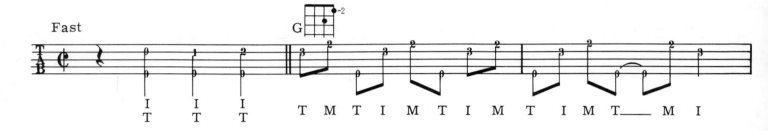

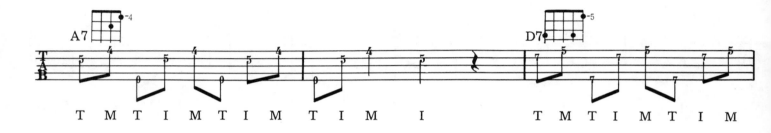

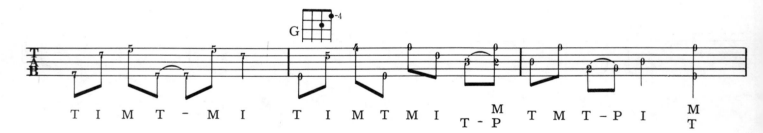

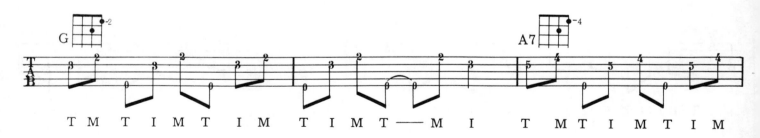

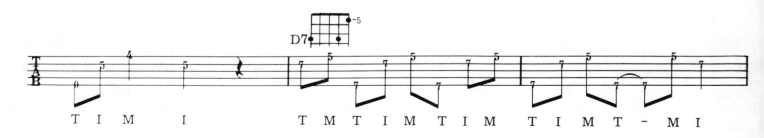

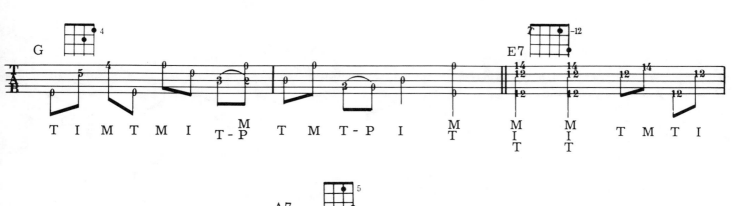
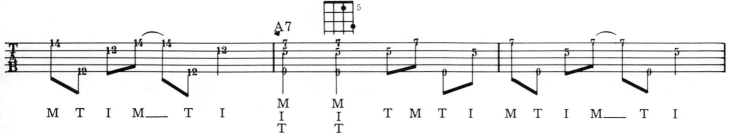
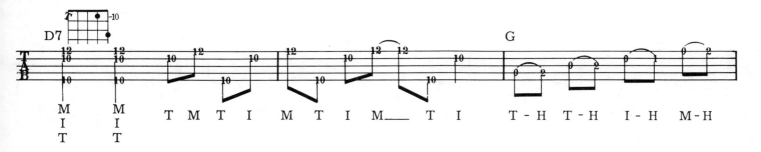
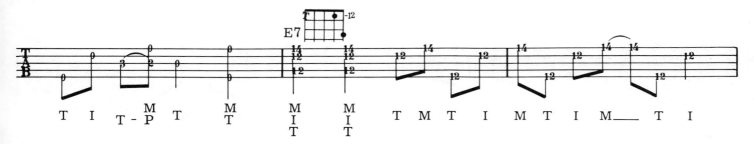
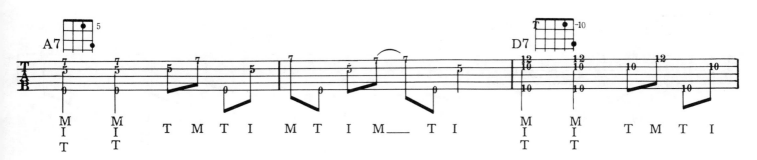

155

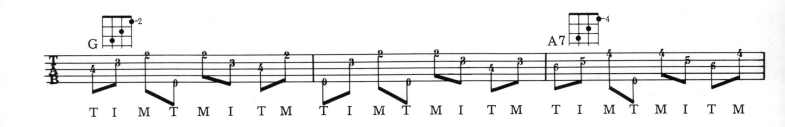

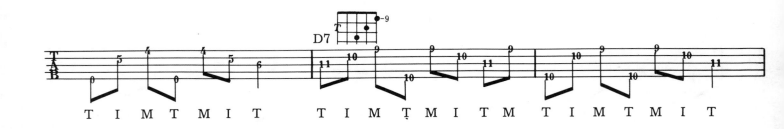

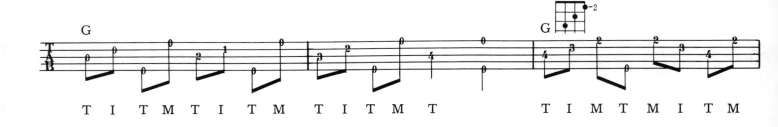

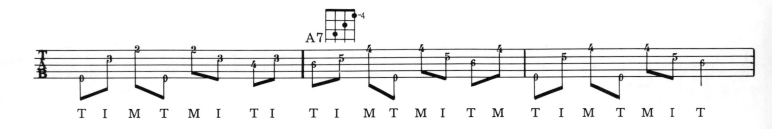

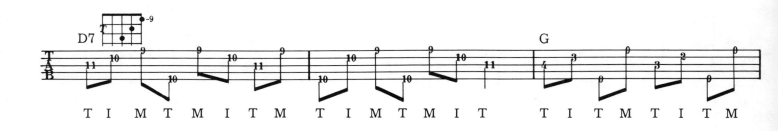

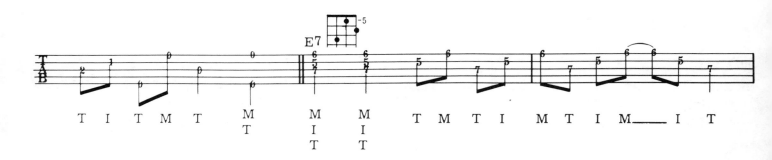

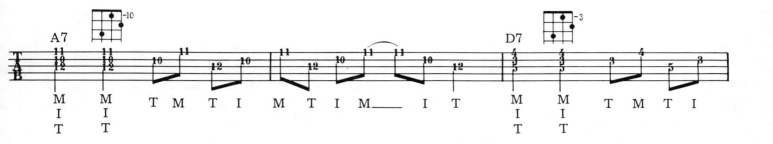

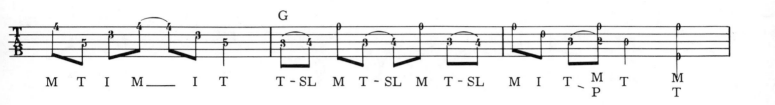

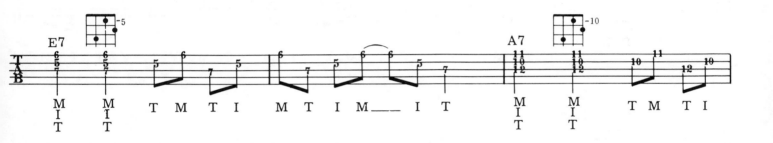

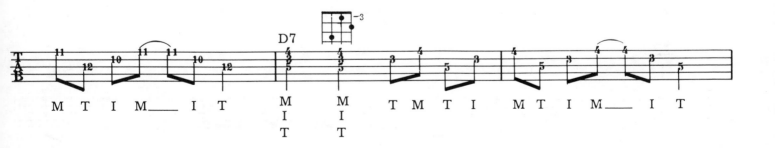

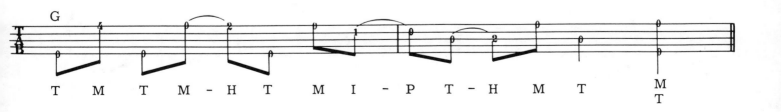

Londonderry Air

Arr. by Neil Griffin

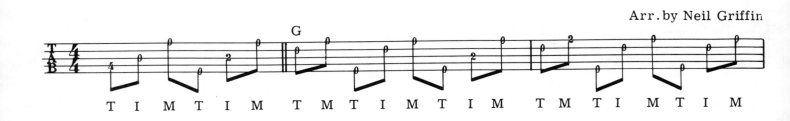

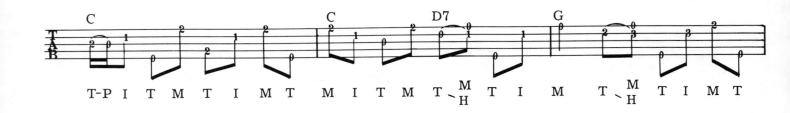

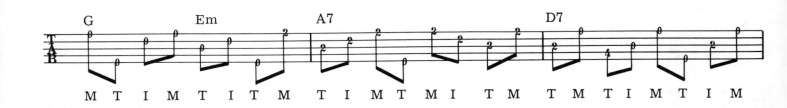

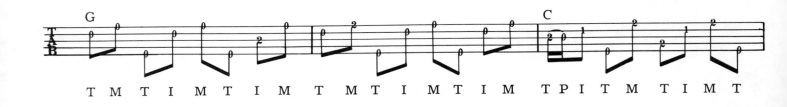

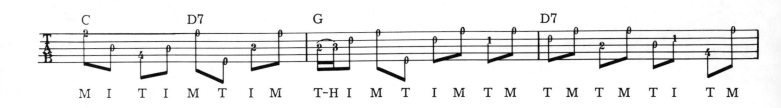

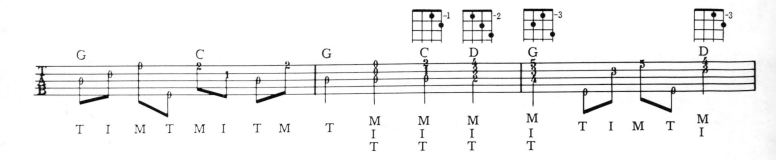

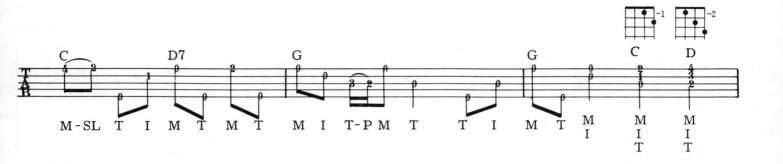

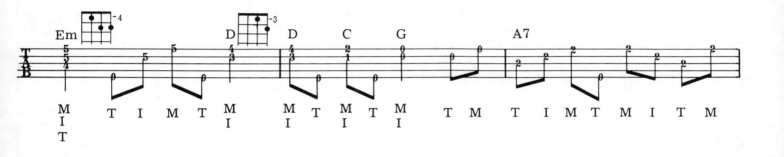

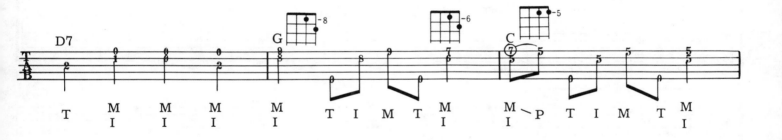

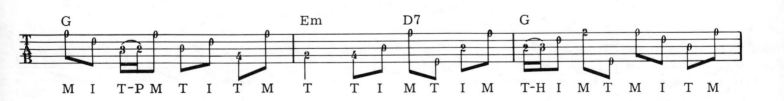

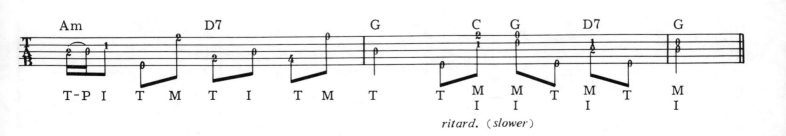

ritard. (*slower*)

St. Anne's Reel

Arr.by:Neil Griffin

160

Under the Double Eagle

ARRANGED BY MARK BARNETT

(REPEAT GOOD ON D.C.)

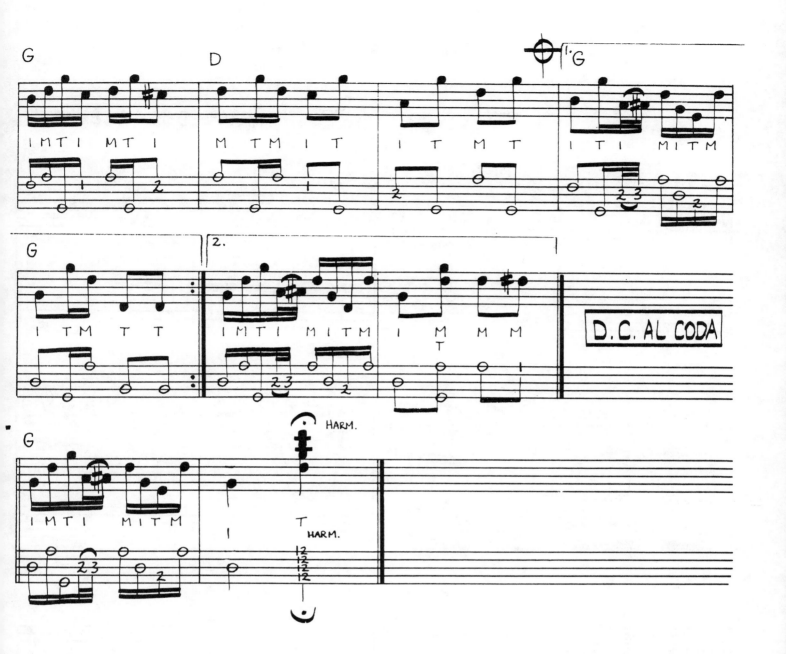

Bill Cheatham

ARRANGED BY MARK BARNETT

164

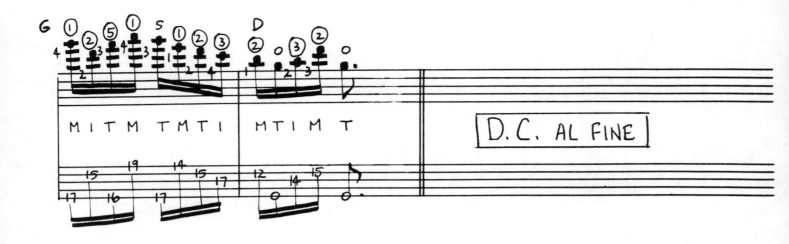

D.C. AL FINE

Temperance Reel

TRANSCRIBED AND ARRANGED BY MARK BARNETT

167

D.C. AL FINE

Dixie

ARRANGED BY MARK BARNETT

STEPHEN FOSTER

170

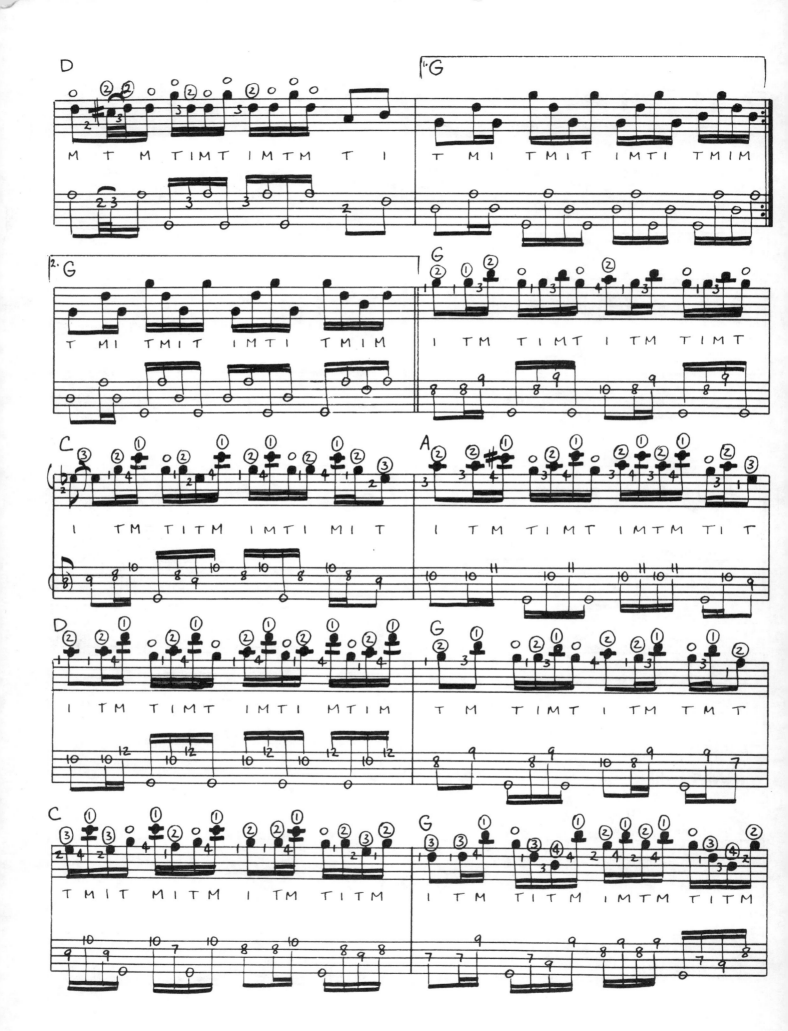

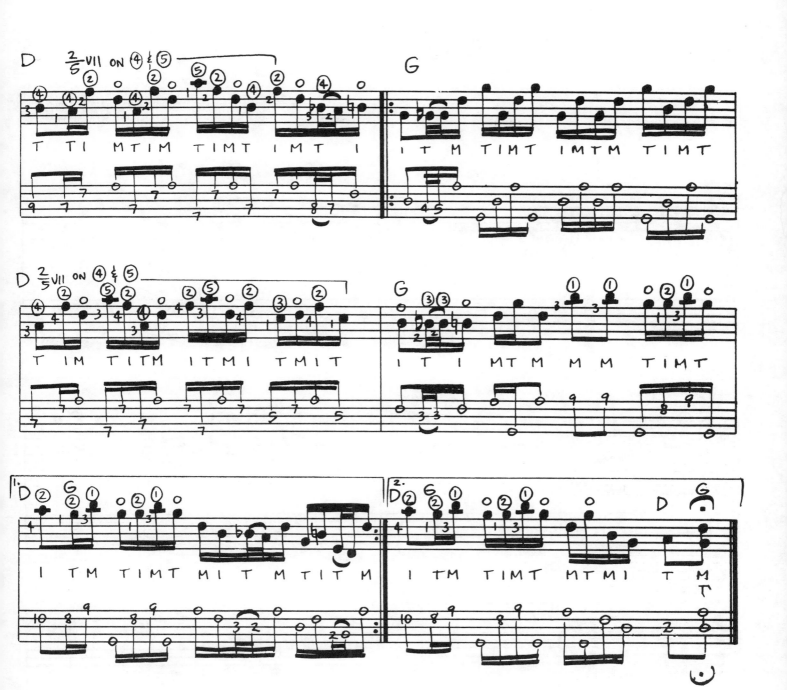

Tom and Jerry

ARRANGED BY MARK BARNETT

FINE

175

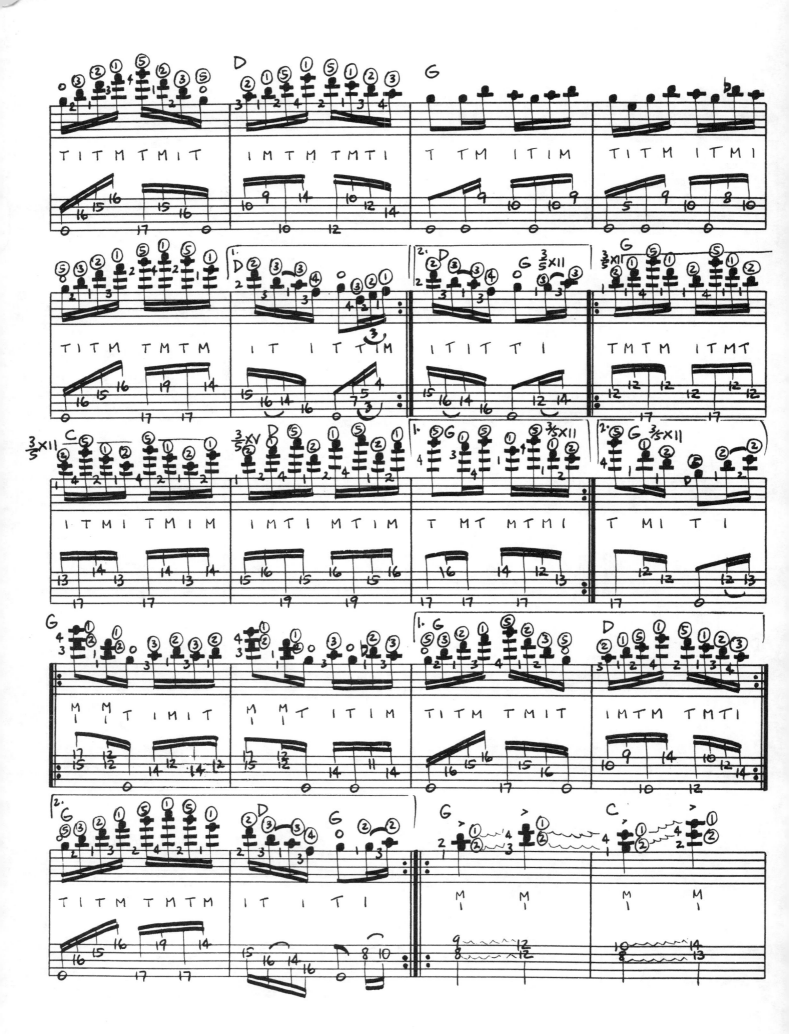

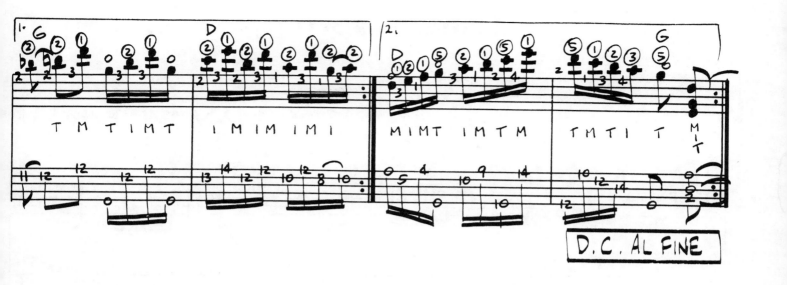

D.C. AL FINE

Fisher's Hornpipe

Transcribed and Arranged by Mark Barnet

178

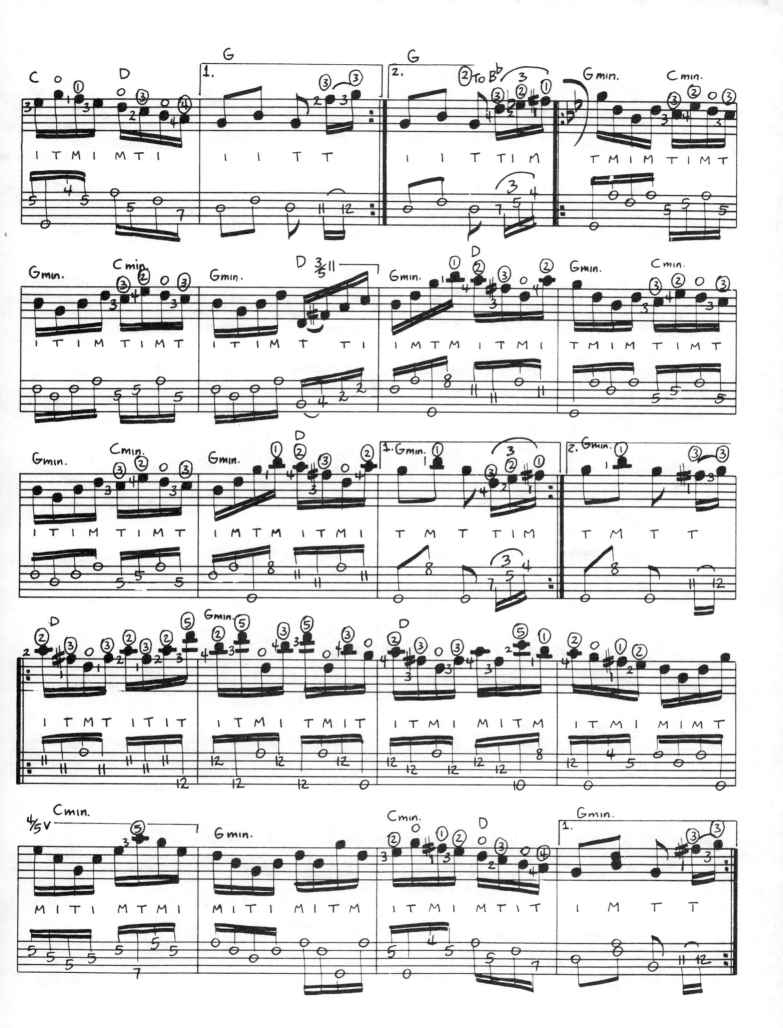

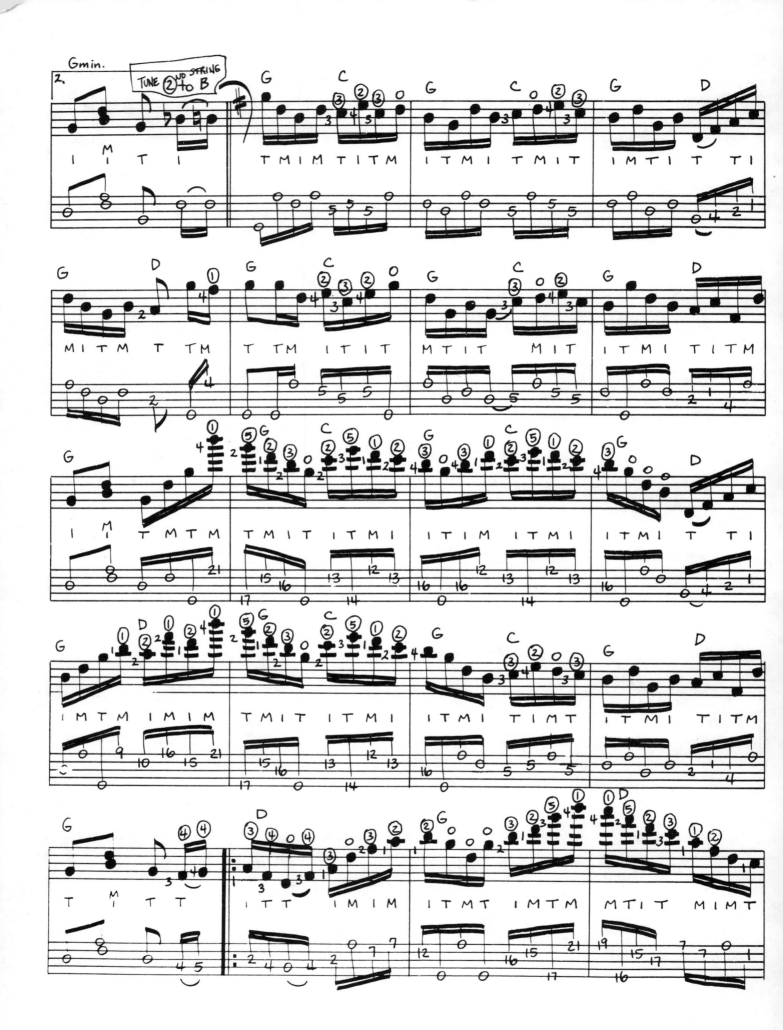

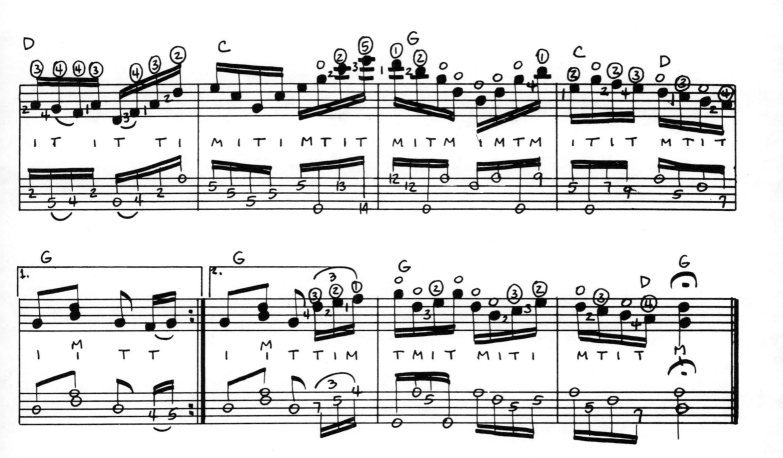